D0219351

Centuries Encircle Me with Fire

Selected Poems of Osip Mandelstam

Centuries Encircle Me with Fire

Selected Poems of Osip Mandelstam

**Translations
by Ian Probstein**

BOSTON
2022

Library of Congress Cataloging-in-Publication Data

Names: Mandel'shtam, Osip, 1891-1938, author. | Probshtein, Ian,
    translator. | Mandel'shtam, Osip, 1891-1938. Stolet'ia okruzhaiut
    menia ognem. English. | Mandel'shtam, Osip, 1891-1938. Stolet'ia
    okruzhaiut menia ognem.
Title: Centuries encircle me with fire: selected poems = Stolet'ia
    okruzhaiut menia ognem: izbrannye stikhotvoreniia / Osip Mandel'stam;
    compiled, translated, and edited by Ian Probstein = Osipa
    Mandel'shtama ; sostavitel' i perevodchik Ian Probshtein.
Description: Bilingual edition = Dvuiazychnoe izdanie. | Boston :
    Academic Studies Press, 2022. | Includes bibliographical references. |
    Parallel texts in Russian and English.
Identifiers: LCCN 2022002988 (print) | LCCN 2022002989 (ebook) |
    ISBN 9781644697160 (hardback) | ISBN 9781644697177 (paperback) |
    ISBN 9781644697184 (adobe pdf) | ISBN 9781644697191 (epub)
Subjects: LCSH: Mandel'shtam, Osip, 1891-1938—Translations into English. |
    LCGFT: Poetry.
Classification: LCC PG3476.M355 C4613 2022 (print) | LCC PG3476.M355
    (ebook) | DDC 891.71/42—dc23/eng/20220204
LC record available at https://lccn.loc.gov/2022002988
LC ebook record available at https://lccn.loc.gov/2022002989

ISBN 9781644697160 (hardback)
ISBN 9781644697177 (paperback)
ISBN 9781644697184 (adobe pdf)
ISBN 9781644697191 (epub)

Copyright © 2022 Academic Studies Press. All rights reserved

Book design by Tatiana Vernikov
Cover design by Ivan Grave

On the cover: a portrait of Osip Mandelstam by Lev Bruni (1916). Reproduced
    by permission.

Published by Academic Studies Press
1577 Beacon Street
Brookline, MA 02446, USA
press@academicstudiespress.com
www.academicstudiespress.com

For my wife Natalia Kazakova and my son Yuri,
great lovers of Osip Mandelstam's poetry and prose,
who encouraged me for many years.

Contents

Acknowledgements 15

A Note on the Text 18

Osip Mandelstam: "Centuries encircle me with fire" 19

On Translating Mandelstam 66

Осип Мандельштам (1891–1938) / Osip Mandelstam (1891–1938)

Из книги «Камень» (стихотворения 1908–1915)
From Stone (poems of 1908–1915)

«Дано мне тело — что мне делать с ним ...» 78
" I am given a body—what should I ..." 79

«Я ненавижу свет ...» 80
"I hate the light ..." 81

«Паденье — неизменный спутник страха ...» 82
"The fall is a constant companion of fear ..." 83

Айя-София 84
Hagia Sophia 85

«... На луне не растет ...» 86
"... Not a single blade ..." 87

Посох 88
The Wand 89

«Уничтожает пламень ...» 90
"The fire destroys ..." 91

Из книги «Tristia» (стихотворения 1916–1922)
From Tristia (poems of 1916–1922)

Декабрист 92
A Decembrist 93

«Когда в тёплой ночи замирает ...» 94
"When a feverish forum of Moscow ..." 95

«Прославим, братья, сумерки свободы . . .» 96
"Hail, brothers, let us praise our freedom's twilight . . ." 97

Tristia 98
Tristia 99

«На каменных отрогах Пиэрии . . .» 100
"On steep stony ridges of Pieria . . ." 101

«Сёстры — тяжесть и нежность, одинаковы ваши приметы . . .» 102
"Sisters, heaviness and tenderness, your traits are akin . . ." 103

«Вернись в смесительное лоно . . .» 104
"Go back to the incestuous womb . . ." 105

«Веницейской жизни, мрачной и бесплодной . . .» 106
"The meaning of fruitless and gloomy . . ." 107

«За то, что я руки твои не сумел удержать . . .» 108
"Because I could not hold your hands in mine . . ." 109

Из книги «Стихотворения»
(1928 г., стихотворения 1921–1925 гг.)
From *Poems*
(1928, poems of 1921–1925)

«С розовой пеной усталости у мягких губ . . .» 110
"With the pink foam of fatigue around soft lips . . ." 111

Век 112
The Age 113

Нашедший подкову 116
The Horseshoe Finder 117

Грифельная ода 122
The Slate Ode 123

«Язык булыжника мне голубя понятней . . .» 128
"Clearer than pigeon's talk to me is stone's tongue . . ." 129

А небо будущим беременно 130
And the Sky is Pregnant with the Future 131

1 января 1924 134
January 1, 1924 135

«Нет, никогда, ничей я не был современник . . .» 140
"No, I've never been anyone's contemporary . . ." 141

«Я буду метаться по табору улицы тёмной…» 142
"I'll rush along a gypsy camp of a dark street…" 143

Из Новых стихотворений 1930–1934 гг.
From *New Poems* of 1930–1934

Армения 144
Armenia 145

1. «Ты розу Гафиза колышешь…» 1. 144
1. "You rock the rose of Hafiz…" 145

2. «Ах, ничего я не вижу, и бедное ухо оглохло…» 146
2. "Ah, I can't see a thing, and my poor ear is deaf…" 147

3. «Ты красок себе пожелала…» 148
3. "You wished colors—and then…" 149

4. «Закутав рот, как влажную розу…» 150
4. "Covering your mouth like a dewy rose…" 151

5. «Руку платком обмотай и в венценосный шиповник…» 150
5. "Wrap your hand in a handkerchief and boldly…" 151

6. «Орущих камней государство…» 152
6. "A country of roaring stones…" 153

7. «Не развалины—нет!—но порубка могучего циркульного леса…» 152
7. "Not ruins—no, but a cutting-down of a mighty circular wood…" . 153

8. «Холодно розе в снегу…» 154
8. "A rose is cold in the snow…" 155

9. «Какая роскошь в нищенском селеньи…» 154
9. "It's such a luxury in a poor village…" 155

10. «О порфирные цокая граниты…» 156
10. "Clanking on regal granites…" 157

11. «Лазурь да глина, глина да лазурь…» 156
11. "Azure and clay, clay and azure skies…" 157

12. «Я тебя никогда не увижу…» 156
12. "I will never see you again…" 157

«На полицейской бумаге верже…» 158
"On the police laid paper the night…" 159

«Не говори никому…» 160
"Don't tell it anyone—forget…" 161

«Колючая речь Араратской долины…» 162
"A prickly speech of the Ararat Valley…" 163

«Как люб мне натугой живущий…» 164
"How dear to me are those people…" 165

«Дикая кошка — армянская речь…» 166
"A wild cat—the Armenian speech…" 167

«Я скажу тебе с последней…» 168
"I will tell you this, my lady…" 169

«За гремучую доблесть грядущих веков…» 170
"For the thunderous courage of ages to come…" 171

«Нет, не спрятаться мне от великой муры…» 172
"No, I won't be able to hide from a great mess…" 173

Неправда 174
Untruth 175

«Полночь в Москве. Роскошно буддийское лето…» 176
"Midnight in Moscow. A Buddhist summer is lavish…" 177

Отрывки из уничтоженных стихов 182
Excerpts from Destroyed Poems 183

   1. «В год тридцать первый от рожденья века…» 182
   1. "On the thirty-first year from this century's birth…" 183

   2. «Уж я люблю московские законы…» 182
   2. "I have already loved Moscow laws…" 183

   3. «Захочешь жить, тогда глядишь с улыбкой…» 184
   3. "If you are thirsty, then look with a smile…" 185

   4. «Я больше не ребенок!…» 184
   4. "I am no longer a child!…" 185

«Ещё далеко мне до патриарха…» 186
"I am far from being as old as patriarch…" 187

«Сегодня можно снять декалькомани…» 190
"Today we can take decals…" 191

Ламарк 194
Lamarck 195

Импрессионизм 198
Impressionism 199

Батюшков 200
Batiushkov 201

«Дайте Тютчеву стрекóзу . . .» 202
"Give Tiutchev a dragonfly . . ." 203

Ариост 204
Ariosto 205

«Не искушай чужих наречий, но постарайся их забыть . . .» 206
"Do not tempt foreign tongues—attempt forgetting them, alas . . ." 207

«Квартира тиха, как бумага . . .» 208
"An apartment is quiet as paper . . ." 209

«Мы живём, под собою не чуя страны . . .» 212
"We live without feeling our country's pulse . . ." 213

Восьмистишия 214
Octaves 215

    1. «Люблю появление ткани . . .» 214
    1. "I love when the substance appears . . ." 215

    2. «Люблю появление ткани . . .» 214
    2. "I love when the substance appears . . ." 215

    3. «О, бабочка, о, мусульманка . . .» 216
    3. "Oh, Moslem-butterfly . . ." 217

    4. «Шестого чувства крошечный придаток . . .» 216
    4. "A tiny appendage of the sixth sense . . ." 217

    5. «Преодолев затверженность природы . . .» 218
    5. "Overcoming the hardiness of nature . . ." 219

    6. «Когда, уничтожив набросок . . .» 218
    6. "When having destroyed your draft . . ." 219

    7. «И Шуберт на воде, и Моцарт в птичьем гаме . . .» 220
    7. "Both Schubert on the water and Mozart in birds' chirping . . ." 221

    8. «И клёна зубчатая лапа . . .» 220
    8. "And the jagged bough of a maple-tree . . ." 221

    9. «Скажи мне, чертёжник пустыни . . .» 222
    9. "Tell me, a draftsman of the desert . . ." 223

    10. «В игольчатых чумных бокалах . . .» 222
    10. "We drink the enchantment of causes . . ." 223

    11. «И я выхожу из пространства . . .» 224
    11. "So I leave space for a wild garden . . ." 225

Стихи памяти Андрея Белого 226
To the Memory of Andrei Bely 227

Утро 10 января 1934 228
The Morning of January 10, 1934 229

    1. «Меня преследуют две-три случайных фразы...» 228
    1. "I am haunted by a couple of random phrases..." 229

    2. «Когда душе столь то́ропкой, столь робкой...» 230
    2. "When a soul, impatient, shy and fast..." 231

    3. «Дышали шуб меха, плечо к плечу теснилось...» 230
    3. "The furs of coats breathed, shoulder to shoulder..." 231

10 января 1934 (вариант 2) 232
January 10, 1934 (version 2) 233

Из Воронежских тетрадей (стихотворения 1935–1937)
From the Voronezh Notebooks (poems of 1935–1937)
Из Первой тетради
From the First Notebook

«Пусти меня, отдай меня, Воронеж...» 236
"Let go, Voronezh, raven-town..." 237

«Я должен жить, хотя я дважды умер...» 236
"I have to live though I died twice..." 237

«Лишив меня морей, разбега и разлёта...» 236
"Having deprived me of seas, flight, and space..." 237

«День стоял о пяти головах. Сплошные пять суток...» 238
"The day was five-headed: five unbreakable days..." 239

«Ещё мы жизнью по́лны в высшей мере...» 240
"We are still sentenced to life..." 241

«Римских ночей полновесные слитки...» 240
"Solid gold bars of the Roman nights..." 241

«За Паганини длиннопалым...» 242
"They run like a gypsy throng..." 243

«Исполню дымчатый обряд...» 244
"I'll fulfill a dim rite..." 245

Из Второй тетради
From the Second Notebook

«Не у меня, не у тебя — у них…» 246
"Not I, not you—but they…" 247

«Улыбнись, ягненок гневный с Рафаэлева холста…» 248
"Smile, angry lamb from Rafael's canvas, don't rage…" 249

«Дрожжи мира дорогие…» 250
"World's golden yeast, our dear…" 251

«Ещё не умер ты, ещё ты не один…» 250
"You haven't died yet. You are not alone…" 251

«Что делать нам с убитостью равнин…» 252
"What should we do with murdered plains…" 253

«Вооружённый зреньем узких ос…» 254
"Armed with the vision of narrow wasps…" 255

Из Третьей тетради
From the Third Notebook

Стихи о неизвестном солдате 256
Verses on the Unknown Soldier 257

«Я молю, как жалости и милости…» 264
"I beg like compassion and grace…" 265

«Я скажу это начерно, шёпотом…» 266
"I will say it in draft and in whisper…" 267

«Может быть, это точка безумия…» 268
"It might be the point of insanity…" 269

«Не сравнивай: живущий несравним…» 270
"A living man's unique: do not compare…" 271

«Чтоб, приятель и ветра и капель…» 272
"To help a friend of rain and wind…" 273

«Гончарами велик остров синий…» 274
"A blue island, green Crete is extolled…" 275

«Длинной жажды должник виноватый…» 276
"A guilty debtor of a long-time thirst…" 277

«О, как же я хочу…» 278
"Oh, how I madly crave…" 279

«Нереиды мои, нереиды!...» 278
"My nereids, oh, my nereids!..." 279

«Флейты греческой тэта и йота...» 280
"Greek flute's theta and iota..." 281

«На меня нацелилась груша да черёмуха...» 282
"I'm under fire of a bird cherry tree and a pear tree..." 283

[Стихи к Н<аталии> Е. Штемпель] 284
[Poems for N<atalia> E. Shtempel] 285

    I. «К пустой земле невольно припадая...» 284
    I. "Unwillingly clinging to a bare land..." 285

    II. «Есть женщины, сырой земле родные...» 284
    II. "Some women are kin to damp earth..." 285

Abbreviations 286

Bibliography 287

  Publications of Works by Osip E. Mandelstam 287

  Translations into English 288

  Translations of Osip Mandelstam's Poems into Other Languages 288

  Criticism 288

Index of poems 297

Acknowledgements

The list of my debts of gratitude is vast, but first and foremost, I want to thank Touro College and President Kadish for granting me a sabbatical to finalize my lifelong research and translation of Osip Mandelstam's poems: in my youth my friends and I retyped Osip Mandelstam's poems using carbon paper, from his *Voronezh Notebooks*, forbidden at that time. I also want to extend my gratitude and thank my publisher, Academic Studies Press, which published my previous book as well. I am extremely grateful to Yuri L'vovich Freidin (1942–2021) who not only gave permission to publish the poems of Osip Mandelstam but also verified the Russian originals; and to Dr. Oleg Lekmanov for midful remarks concerning the Russian texts. I would also like to thank Charles Bernstein and Jerome Rothenberg for their encouragement and support, and my son Yuri Probstein-Kazakov for some insightful remarks concerning some of my translations. I am grateful to the editors of periodicals listed below where my translations of Osip Mandelstam's poems have been first published.

Several translations and a somewhat different essay on Osip Mandelstam's poetry were published in my book *The River of Time: Time-Space, Language and History in Avant-Garde, Modernist, and Contemporary Poetry* (Boston: Academic Studies Press, 2017).[1]

My translations of Osip Mandelstam's poems "The Horseshoe Finder," "The Age," and "January 1, 1924" were finalists for the Gabo (Gabriel Marquez) Prize for translation and multilingual texts. They appeared in *Lunch Ticket* (Summer/Fall 2016), a literary and art journal Antioch University's MFA program.[2]

My article "On the Translations of Osip Mandelstam's 'Stalin's Epigram'" was originally published in *Jacket 2*, August 11, 2014.[3]

---

1   Available online at: https://www.academicstudiespress.com/jewsofrussiaeasterneurope/the-river-of-time?rq=The%20River%20of%20Time.

2   http://lunchticket.org/the-horseshoe-finder/.

3   http://jacket2.org/commentary/ian-probstein-mandelstam-stalin-epigram.

My translation of Osip Mandelstam's «Неправда» [Untruth] appeared in *Sibylla* (Rio de Janeiro, Brasil), August 10, 2014.[4]

The article "Fear and Awe: On Osip Mandelstam's 'The Slate Ode'" and my translation of "The Slate Ode" into English appeared in *Brooklyn Rail: In Translation* (March 2011).[5]

My translation of Osip Mandelstam's "The Octaves" appeared in *Brooklyn Rail: In Translation* (March 2011).[6]

My translations of Osip Mandelstam's poems "I'll Rush Along a Gypsy Camp of a Dark Street," and "They Run like a Gypsy Crowd" were published in *CrazyHorse* 80 (Fall 2011): 87–89.

My translations of Osip Mandelstam's poem «Стихи о неизвестном солдате» [Verses on the Unknown Soldier] and of other poems: «Я прошу, как жалости и милости» [I Beg Like Compassion and Grace . . .], «Я скажу это начерно—шёпотом . . .» [I will Say It in Draft, in a Whisper . . .], «Может быть, это точка безумия . . .» [It Might be the Point of Insanity . . .], «Чтоб приятель и ветра и капель . . .» [To Help a Friend of Wind and Rain . . .], «На меня нацелилась груша, да черёмуха . . .» [I'm under Fire of a Bird Cherry and a Pear Tree . . .] were published in *Four Centuries of Russian Poetry in Translation* 4 (2013): 14–20.[7]

My translations of Osip Mandelstam's "Hagia Sophia" and "Impressionism" were published in *Osip Mandelstam: New Translations*, ed. Ilya Bernstein (New York: UDP, 2006), 6 and 19.

My translations of Osip Mandelstam's cycle *Armenia* and other poems were first published in *The International Literary Quarterly* 13, no. 2 (2011).[8]

My translations of Osip Mandelstam's "To the Memory of Andrei Bely," "January 10, 1934," "When a Soul, Shy and Fast," "He Conducted the Orchestra of the Caucasian peaks," "Amidst the Crowd, Bearded and Deep in Thought" were published in *Four Centuries of Russian Poetry* 3 (2012).[9]

---

4   http://sibila.com.br/english/osip-mandelstam-untruth/10871.

5   http://intranslation.brooklynrail.org/russian/the-slate-ode.

6   http://intranslation.brooklynrail.org/russian/octaves-and-other-poems-by-osip-mandelstam.

7   http://www.perelmuterverlag.de/FC42013.pdf.

8   http://www.interlitq.org/issue13-2/osip-mandelstam/job.php.

9   http://www.perelmuterverlag.de/FC32012.pdf.

My translation of Osip Mandelstam's poem "Lamarck" was first published in *Metamorphoses* 20, no. 1 (Spring 2012): 76–79.

My translation of four poems: "Hagia Sophia," "I will Say It in Draft, in a Whisper," "Armed with a Vision of Narrow Wasps," "I will Tell You This, My Lady," appeared in *International Poetry Review* 30, no. 2 (Fall 2004): 64–69.

A Note on the Text

My Russian texts for the translation and citations have been verified against the splendid and thoroughful editions: Osip Mandel'shtam, *Polnoe sobraniie sochinenii i pisem* [Complete works and letters], 3 vols., comp. and ed. A. G. Mets (Moscow: Progress and Pleiada, 2010); and idem, *Sobranie stikhotvorenii 1906–1937* [Collected Poems 1906–1937], comp. Oleg Lekmanov and Maksim Amelin (Moscow: Ruteniia, 2017).

Osip Mandelstam: "Centuries encircle me with fire"

The great Russian poet Osip Mandelstam (1891–1938) led an unsettled life full of tribulations, wandering and exile. After his Stalin epigram of 1933, the dictator, who used to say that "vengeance is best when served cold," never forgave the poet: Mandelstam was sent to Cherdyn' in Siberia. Afterwards, due to the protection of Bukharin, then a powerful Communist party functionary who was fond of Mandelstam's poetry, the term was somewhat softened: Mandelstam had to live in the provincial town of Voronezh, deprived of the right to live in the capital and big cities. He was finally arrested again in 1937 and sent to the so-called Vladivostok transition camp Vtoraya Rechka [Second River], waiting to be transferred to the main Gulag Camp. The prisoners were transported by freight cars or box cars, and the way from Moscow to Vladivostok took more than a month. When Mandelstam arrived, he was already emaciated and sick. According to the witnesses, when Mandelstam was in a good mood, he would read the poems of Baudelaire and Verlain in French, Dante and Petrarch in Italian, and would also read Balmont's, Briusov's and his own translations. However, in the camp, he developed a mania that someone would poison him. He would grab a ration before they were officially distributed, for which he was beaten up. When a doctor, a fellow prisoner, examined Mandelstam, he said that he would not last long, and it was a matter of several weeks if not less when the poet would die. Osip Mandelstam perished on December 27, 1938, and was buried there in a communal grave.[1]

Having gone through all the circles of earthly hell and purgatory, anticipating his own arrest and perhaps death, Mandelstam nevertheless claims that

---

1   *Letopis' zhizni i tvorchestva O. E. Mandel'stama*, comp. A. G. Mets, S. V. Vasilenko, L. M. Vidgof, D. I. Zubarev, E. I. Lubiannikova, P. Mitzner (St. Petersburg: n. p., 2019), 468–471. Hereafter, *Letopis'*.

heaven is a "lifetime home," thus creating his own form of *paradiso terrestre* ("earthly paradise," as Pound put it in Italian in *The Cantos*). In his later poem of 1937, Mandelstam wrote:

> I will say it in draft, in a whisper—
> Since the time has not come yet:
> The game of the instinctive heaven
> Is attained through experience and sweat.
>
> And beneath a temporal sky
> Of purgatory we often forget
> That this happy heaven's depot
> Is our expanding and lifetime homestead.
> *(1937; translation here and further is mine, if not noted otherwise)*

Mandelstam does not see a contradiction between nature and eternity and, unlike the great Irish poet William Butler Yeats, never dreams of departing from nature; he even feels inferior to it.

> Ne u menia, ne u tebia—u nikh
> Vsia sila okonchanii rodovykh . . .
> [It's not I, not you—it's they
> Who have the entire strength of gender (ancestral) endings.[2]]

In his usual manner, Mandelstam simultaneously implies several meanings in the word "rodovoi": "ancestral," "genus," and "generic," thus alluding to being and procreation as well as to creativity. He then states that "porous reeds are singing naturally in the wind, / and the snails of human lips [the metaphor speaks for itself] / will gratefully absorb their breathing heaviness." Mandelstam urges one (addressing himself rather than his readers) "to enter their cartilage— / and you will be the heir of their kingdoms. // And for humans, for their living hearts / Wandering in their curves and twists, / You will picture both their pleasures / And the pain that tortures them in time of tides."[3] On another occasion, he wrote: "Na podvizhnoi lestnitse Lamarka /

---

2   Interlinear translation is mine. For the literary translation see p. 247.

3   Here I give an interlinear translation; see also the translation of this poem of 1936 in the *Second Voronezh Notebook*. Mandelstam uses the second person singular here in place of the first person. The specific role of personal pronouns in the structure of the poetic text was profoundly analyzed by Roman Iakobson, "Poeziia grammatiki i grammatika poezii,"

Ia zaimu posledniuiu stupen'"[4] [On Lamarck's flexible scale / I will take the lowest stair], alluding to Jean Baptiste Lamarck's (1744–1829) theory of organic evolution, which Mandelstam openly admired both in his poetry and in prose: "Lamarck feels the rifts between classes. He hears the pauses and syncopes of the evolutionary line." Earlier, Mandelstam noted, "In Lamarck's reversed, descending movement down the ladder of living creatures resides the greatness of Dante. The lower forms of organic existence are humanity's Inferno."[5] "Inferno" is the key word. If memory, progress, the refined human intellect do not matter, it is better to lose memory and perhaps humanity to escape the horror of contemporary life:

> If all living nature is but an error
> Of a short nightmarish day,
> I will take the lowest stair
> On Lamark's flexible scale.

Now the stanza acquires a different connotation due to the if-clause and the epithet "nightmarish." The poem seems to be about Lamarck's theory of organic evolution, but is really a sharp protest against the poet's contemporary life:

> He says that nature abounds in fractures,
> There's no vision—you see for the last time.
>
> He says: "The resonance will cease,
> You loved Mozart in vain:
> A spider's deafness will seize
> You—this gap is beyond our gain."

Nadezhda Mandelstam wrote in her "Comments to the Poems of 1930–1937" that in "Lamarck" and in "Octaves" 8 and 9 there is "a horrible fall of human beings who forgot Mozart and denied everything (mind, vision, hearing) in that kingdom of spider-like deafness."[6] In the "nightmarish" Soviet life of

in *Poetyca* (Warsaw: Polska Akademia Nauk, Instytut Badań Literackich, and Państwowe Wydawnictwo Naukove, 1961), 405, 409; see also Iurii Lotman, "Zametki po poetike Tiutcheva," in *O poetakh i poezii* (St. Petersburg: Iskusstvo, 1996), 553–564.

4   Osip Mandel'shtam, *Polnoe sobranie sochinenii i pisem*, comp. and ed. A. G. Mets (Moscow: Progress-Pleyada, 2010), 1:171.

5   Osip Mandelstam, *The Complete Critical Prose and Letters*, ed. Jane Gary Harris, trans. J. G. Harris and Constance Link (Ann Arbor: Ardis, 1979), 367 (hereafter CPL).

6   Nadezhda Mandel'shtam, *Tret'ia kniga* (Moscow: Agraf, 2006), 283 (translation is mine).

that time, there was no need either for vision or hearing; therefore, there was no need for art or music. Naturally, it is Mandelstam, not Lamarck, who bitterly exclaims: "You loved Mozart in vain." In contemporary life as Mandelstam observed it, only primitive types could survive. There was no more need for the "uninterrupted procession of generations," as Przybylsky observed while analyzing Mandelstam's 1912 poem "Hagia Sophia."[7] Reading "Lamarck," one might even suppose that there is no need for humanity at all. At the end of "Lamarck," written twenty years after "Hagia Sophia," the poet makes gloomy predictions:

> Nature has turned away
> As if she didn't need us anymore
> And put our medulla, spinal cord,
> In a dark sheath like a sword.
>
> She was late or just forgot
> To put down a drawbridge for those
> Who have a green grave,
> A lithe laughter and red breath.

I would not agree completely with the poet's wife, however, that "The Octaves" have the same connotations as "Lamarck." In my view, in "The Octaves," the poet summons the strength and willpower to preserve cultural memory and bridge its gaps and breaks, name the unnamed and thus overcome the infernal state of oblivion:

> A tiny appendage of the sixth sense
> Or lizard's parietal eye,
> Monasteries of snails and shells,
> And a hum of flickering cilia nearby.
>
> Inaccessible—how close, but try to unfold—
> One can neither see it, nor unbind,
> As if a note from somebody you hold
> And it should be immediately replied.
> ("The Octaves" 4)

---

7   Ryszard Przybylski, *An Essay on the Poetry of Osip Mandelstam: God's Grateful Guest* (Ann Arbor: Ardis, 1987), 109.

Therefore, the poet's duty is to reveal the joys and pains of unnamed and unconscious creatures, that is, to name the unnamed. As was correctly noted by Vladimir Toporov,

> The poet [...] gives his reader the gift of what is preserved in his ancestral memory, which in the rarest cases binds the child to something that existed before civilization, before speech and even before birth with that foundation ("S pervoosnovoi zhizni slito" [merged with the foundation of life]) that is the content and meaning of these "recollections" explicated from chaos.[8]

Hence the duty of the poet is to connect human, organic, and even non-organic nature to make order out of chaos and to name the unnamed.

Mandelstam writes about the theory of evolution both in his poetry and prose. In his essay "To the Problem of the Scientific Style of Darwin" (1932), Mandelstam links Darwin's theory of evolution with the discoveries of Linnaeus and Lamarck. This essay can be viewed as an outline for his poems "Lamarck," "It's Not I, Not You—It's They / Who Have the Entire Strength of the Gender [Ancestral] Endings" and the "Monasteries of snails and shells" from "The Octaves."

Written in exile in Voronezh, Mandelstam's late work reveals his anxiety and his desire to overcome loneliness and separation from life in three major ways. As Mikhail Gasparov observed, Mandelstam considered himself a member of the fourth estate, and, therefore, unlike Marina Tsvetaeva, he was not initially proud of being an outcast. And further: "Following the tradition of the fourth estate did not allow Mandelstam to think that all the others are marching out of step, and he alone marches in step."[9] Hence, his first way to overcome separation and exile was by seeking forgiveness and attempting repentance in the so-called Stalin's "Ode," "Stanzas" ("The Heart Needs to Beat"), and the like. The second way Mandelstam tried to overcome the loneliness of exile was by expressing his thirst for life and his acute feeling and vision of life itself. In addition to "Lamarck's flexible scale" and the poems of this cycle mentioned

---

8   Vladimir N. Toporov, *Mif. Ritual. Simvol. Obraz. Issledovaniia v oblasti mifopoeticheskogo* (Moscow: Progress, 1995), 435 (translation is mine).

9   Cf. Mikhail L. Gasparov, *Grazhdanskaia lirika Mande'shtama 1937* (Moscow: Rossiiskii gosudarstvennyi gumanitarnyi universitet, 1996), 18.

above, there is one particular poem reminiscent of Pound's *The Pisan Cantos*, especially Canto 83.

Pound:

> And brother Wasp is building a very neat house
> Of four rooms, one shaped like a squat indian bottle
> (C. 83/532)

Mandelstam:

> Armed with the vision of narrow wasps
> Sucking the axis of the earth, the axis of the earth,
> I feel all that I have had to watch
> And recollect by heart and in vain.
> [...]
> Oh, if only an air's barb and summer warmth
> Could help me to avoid both sleep and death
> And could have made me hear hence
> The axis of the earth, the axis of the earth ...
> (1937)

In addition to the literal affinities with Pound ("the barb of air" and "the barb of time"), the image of the wasp in Mandelstam's case is also an allusion to his—and Stalin's—first name: Iosif-Osip-Osia; the word "wasp" in Russian is *osa*. In the genitive plural it is *os*, while the word denoting earth's axis is a soft and palatalized *os'*, almost a homophone. As Taranovsky observed, there is a hidden allusion here to these lines of the slightly earlier Stalin's "Ode": "I would say who moved the axis of the earth, / honoring the tradition of hundred forty nations."[10] Thus Mandelstam implies all the meanings mentioned above and rhymes them, expressing his anxiety and thirst for life. The poet both begs and rebels:

> Let go, Voronezh, raven-town,
> Let me be, don't let me down,
> You'll drop me, crop me, won't revive,
> Voronezh—whim, Voronezh—raven, knife.
> (April 1935)

---

10 Kiril Taranovsky, *Essays on Mandelstam* (Cambridge, MA and London: Harvard UP, 1976), 113.

A month later, Mandelstam writes:

Having deprived me of seas, flight, space,
You gave me a foothold of a forcible land,
What have you gained? A brilliant end:
You couldn't have taken moving lips away.
(May 1935)[11]

Mandelstam perceives his Voronezh exile as "a lion's den"—"Ia
v l'vinyi rov i v krepost' pogruzhën" [I've been submerged in a lion's den and
a fortress][12]—alluding to the Book of Daniel. Even there, he is longing for life
and thinking of an earthly paradise. He appeals to France: "I beg as compassion and grace, / Your earth and your honeysuckle, France." In this poem, the
Russian poet asserts that "a violet is still a violet in a prison cell."

The third way Mandelstam attempts to overcome his forceful separation
from life is through his "nostalgia for world culture," his search for the harmony of France, Italy, the Mediterranean and "the blessed islands." Here again,
there is affinity between Mandelstam and Pound in the admiration of both
poets for François Villon. Mandelstam writes:

Spitting at the spider's rights,
An impudent scholar, a stealing angel,
Played tough tricks near Gothic sites.
Unrivaled Villon François.

He is a heavenly robber,
It is not shameful to sit near him:
Skylarks will still ring and warble
Before the end of the world... [13]
(1937)

Like Pound in "Montcorbier, Alias Villon," Mandelstam in his essay on
Villon emphasizes Villon's medievalism, his ability to combine both plaintiff
and defendant within his own persona, his self-compassion, which lacks either
self-pity or self-centeredness. Most importantly, Mandelstam writes of Villon's

---

11   Translations are mine.

12   Mandel'shtam, *Polnoe sobranie sochinenii i pisem*, 1:227.

13   Translation is mine.

desire for reality, his denial of abstract notions and his ability to combine gaunt reality with a vision of the divine. Similarly, Pound states that Villon "is utterly mediæval, yet his poems mark the end of mediæval literature [...] he recognizes the irrevocable, he blames no one but himself"[14] and "his poems are gaunt as the *Poema del Cid* is gaunt; they treat of actualities, they are unattained with fancy; in the *Cid* death is death, war is war. In Villon filth is filth, crime is crime; neither crime nor filth is gilded."[15]

Mandelstam feels sympathy for "the heavenly robber," finally associating himself with outcasts and exiles, alluding to Ovid, Dante, and Villon. There is the motif of wandering as exile and a spiritual kinship with Ovid, and through Ovid, with Pushkin, who also addressed his poem to the Roman poet ("To Ovid," 1821) from his Southern exile, as was noted by Przybylski.[16] Such poems as "On the Stony Spurs of Pieria" (1919) and especially, "Thalassa and Thanatos of Grecian Flutes" (1937) reveal Mandelstam's nostalgia for a natural life in an unnatural totalitarian state. There is a certain antagonism and an attempt to escape Soviet reality, not his own human nature. He strives for the "blessed islands" and a time where "no one eats broken bread / Where there is only honey, wine, and milk, / Where a screechy labor does not cloud the sky, / And the turns of the wheel are light."[17] As was brilliantly demonstrated by Przybylski, Mandelstam longs for the islands of the Greek Archipelago, going as far back as Hesiod's *Theogonia* in which the dance of the Muses, born in Pieria, is shown. To be exact, the Muses descended from the mountains of Helicon to the valleys[18] (among them the valley of Tempe in the land Phaecia, Ulysses's last stop on his way home and the probable site of the town from Keats's "Ode on a Grecian Urn"). Przybylski states that Hölderlin called these islands beloved, Byron, "Blessed Isles" and "Leconte de Lisle did not hesitate to call the archipelago holy."[19] Hence, Mandelstam's nostalgia for world culture

---

14 Ezra Pound, *The Spirit of Romance* (Norfolk, CT: New Directions, 1953), 170–171.

15 Ibid., 172–173.

16 Ryszard Przybylski, "Rim Osipa Mandel'shtama," in *Mandel'shtam i antichnost'* (Moscow: Rossiiskii gosudarstvennyi gumanitarnyi universitet, 1995), 44.

17 "Na kamennykh otrogakh Pierii," in Mandel'shtam, *Polnoe sobranie sochinenii i pisem*, 1:105.

18 Przybylski, *An Essay on the Poetry of Osip Mandelstam*, 175–178.

19 Ibid., 187.

is mixed with his longing for the "holy isles," first in 1919 and later in his Voronezh exile in 1937:

> Give me mine back, blue isle,
> Winged Crete, give my toil back,
> And let a flowing goddess fertile
> Breastfeed a glazed vessel's ache . . .
>
> This was and sung with a blue chime
> Long before Odyssey's time,
> Long before food and drink
> Was called "yours" and "mine."

On the other hand, as Efim Etkind observed, Mandelstam's seemingly humorous poem of 1931, "Ia skazhu tebe s poslednei priamotoi" [I will tell you with the last (ultimate) frankness] expresses his bitterness and disillusionment in his quest for "world civilization":

> I will tell you this, my lady,
> With final candor,
> All is folly—sherry-brandy,
> Oh, my angel.
>
> Where Beauty shone
> To a Hellene,
> Disgrace gazed at me
> From a black hole.
>
> Greeks stole Helen
> Along the sea,
> While I taste a salty brine
> On my lips.
>
> Void will soil my lips
> And disgrace,
> Poverty will cock a grim snook
> At my face.[20]
> *(1931)*

---

20   Translation is mine.

Etkind presumes that this poem of 1931 is "Mandelstam's esthetic self-denial: Beauty, which was the purport of art and being, has not endured the test of time and life; it turned out to be a common ugliness, Achaian men turned ordinary Greeks, who, like vulgar criminals, just kidnapped Helen."[21] In my view, Etkind oversimplifies Mandelstam's "self-denial": it is rather a denial of the conditions in which beauty becomes ugliness. The motive of this poem is concealed bitterness disguised as mockery at breaking with world culture when time is "out of joint." Moreover, as was stated by Nadezhda Mandelstam, the poem was written "during a drinking party [*popoika*] in the Zoological Museum,"[22] and therefore cannot be interpreted as a serious refutation of any previous ideas or as "an esthetic self-denial." In his 1937 poem, "Zabludilsia ia v nebe—chto delat'?" [I got lost in heaven—what's to be done?], Mandelstam reveals his metaphysical as well as physical fear. It was easier for those who, like Dante, were close to heaven and God; we are unable to have the same feelings towards God, heaven, and humans, as Dante had. In his thirst for life, threatened by real death, perhaps execution, Mandelstam denies the "sharp-tender laurel" striving for "Florentine nostalgia." (He uses the same word *toská*, with which he expressed his thirst for world culture.) In the other version of the same poem, the *dvoichatka*, as Nadezhda Mandelstam called them, or "twin poem," to use the term of Kiril Taranovsky,[23] the poet begs an unnamed cup-bearer (perhaps the one who deprived him of the cup at the feast of his forefathers in "Za gremuchuiu doblest'") "to give him the strength to drink to the health of the turning tower, / a wrestling crazy azure."[24]

As many scholars of Mandelstam (the most important and profound works are by Kiril Taranovsky, Omry Ronen, Mikhail Gasparov, and Irina

---

21   Efim Etkind, "Osip Mandel'shtam—Trilogiia o veke," in *Zhizn' i tvorchestvo O. E. Mandel'shtama* (Voronezh: Voronezhskii gosudarstvennyi universitet, 1990), 241 (translation is mine).

22   Nadezhda Mandel'shtam, "Kommentarii k stikham 1930–1937 gg.," in *Zhizn' i tvorchestvo O. E. Mandel'shtama* (Voronezh: Voronezhskii gosudarstvennyi universitet, 1990), 199.

23   Cf. Kiril Taranovsky, "Tri zametki o poezii Mandel'shtama," *International Journal of Slavic Linguistics and Poetics* 12 (1969): 167; Nadezhda Mandel'shtam, *Vospominaniia*, in her *Hope against Hope* (New York: Charles Scribner, 1970), 200–216; Omry Ronen, "Lexical Repetition, Subtext and Meaning in Osip Mandelstam's Poetics," *Slavic Poetics Essays in Honor of Kiril Taranovsky*, ed. Roman Jakobson, C. H. van Schooneveld, and Dean S. Worth (Paris: Mouton, 1973), 370.

24   Taranovsky, "Tri zametki o poezii Mandel'shtama," 167.

Semenko[25]) have stated, Mandelstam's poetry is extremely esoteric and is built upon hidden allusions and associations with Russian, European, and classical poetry. Here again, Mandelstam's affinity with Pound and T. S. Eliot and their thirst for world culture is quite evident. Yet, already in "The Age," "January 1, 1924," and other Mandelstam's poems of this period, a strong longing for contemporaneity can also be felt in the verses of this "aging son of a century." Thus, the poem "And the sky is pregnant with the future," published only in the periodical *Lët* [Flying] in 1923, is Mandelstam's highly metaphorical response to multiple political conferences, such as the Genoa conference, the Hague conference, and finally the Rapallo Peace Treaty of 1922, as the result of which the Red Army started to build its air force. On the other hand, "the winners / Walking around the flights's graveyards / Crushed the wings of the dragonflies / And slayed them with little hammers" refers to the provisions of the Treaty of Versailles of 1919, according to which, Germany was forbidden to have an air force and other military equipment.[26]

Likewise, in "January 1, 1924" Mandelstam not only responds to contemporary life but he also defamiliarizes reality, folklore, and current events. Thus, he connects a fairy tale about a lazy Ivan whose wishes are miraculously fulfilled by the pike ("by the pike's order and my wish") while he remains lying on his warm couch-stove, with an allusion to the satirical fable "Carp-Idealist" of the great Russian satirist Mikhail Saltykov-Shchedrin (1826–1889). In the story, Carp was proclaiming ideas of equality, observing the laws, which were labeled as "socialist," and in the end, called for a dispute with Pike, was later taken in custody and finally eaten, or, rather, occasionally swallowed by the Pike. In addition to satire and fairy tales, Mandelstam adds another "fish metaphor": "It rattles with frozen fish, streams steam / Like silver roach-fish from rosy tearooms," alluding to the hunger of 1920s.

However, Yuri Tynianov, in his essay dedicated to modern Russian poetry, "Promezhutok" ["The gap" or "The space between"], writes about the "bloom" of contemporary Russian prose and the "decline" of poetry in the 1920s.

---

25   See, among others, Kiril Taranovsky, *Essays on Mandelstam* (Cambridge, MA: Harvard UP, 1976); Gasparov, *Grazhdanskaia lirika Mandel'shtama*; I. M. Semenko, *Poetika pozdnego Mandel'shtama* (Moscow: Mandel'shtamovskoe obshchestvo, 1997).

26   See Oleg Lekmanov's comment to this poem in Osip Mandel'shtam, *Sobranie stikhotvorenii 1906–1937*, comp. Oleg Lekmanov and Maksim Amelin (Moscow: Ruteniia, 2017), 400.

Comparing the poetry of Pasternak and Mandelstam, Tynianov writes that "a word in Pasternak's work becomes an almost palpable thing, while in Mandelstam a thing becomes an abstraction [a versified abstraction]."[27] Tynianov continues that the peculiarity of Mandelstam's poetry is that it has "not a word, but shades of words and meanings," and that his work resembles "the work of almost a foreigner in the literary language."[28] This was probably to some extent true as far as Mandelstam's first book *Kamen'* [Stone] of 1913 was concerned, but Tynianov's essay was written after "January 1, 1924" had been published, and this text, together with Mandelstam's great poems of 1923 ("The Slate Ode," "The Horseshoe Finder"), proves that the poet was also seeking reality, is overlooked by Tynianov.

Pasternak is—and was—contemporary, real; his thirst for life (*Life, My Sister* is the title of one of his books) at that point in his work was satisfied by contemporary reality, by the present moment. He rarely went farther back (even in his long "epic" poems), than "1905" or the nineteenth century. In my view, Mandelstam, in his "Verses on the Unknown Soldier" discussed below, managed to express his own time as well as the timeless more profoundly and impressively than Pasternak. Mandelstam also claimed to be a contemporary: "It's time you knew: I'm a contemporary too." I would argue that both Mandelstam's theoretical views and his art of that period ("The Age," "January 1, 1924," and his later poems, especially those of his Moscow and Voronezh period, 1935–1937) prove that he too was seeking reality, life.

In opposition to Viacheslav Ivanov's slogan, *a realibus ad realiora* ["from the real to the most real"], as stated in Ivanov's 1909 book of essays, *By the Stars,* Mandelstam in "Utro Akmeizma" ("The Morning of Acmeism" of 1914) expressed his understanding of reality and realism by means of a mathematical equation, "A=A—what a magnificent theme for poetry! Symbolism languished and yearned for the law of identity. Acmeism made it its slogan and proposed its adoption instead of the ambiguous *a realibus ad realiora.*"[29] Notably, in this search for reality and "making it new," both Pound and Mandelstam turned to the Middle Ages and to Provence. Mandelstam wrote in "The Morning of Acmeism" (1914; according to Mets, the author's date of 1912 is not exact; it was most probably, the end of 1913–the beginning of 1914: based on

---

27 Iurii Tynianov, *Poetika. Istoriia literatury. Kino* (Moscow: Nauka, 1977), 189.

28 Ibid., 190–191.

29 Mandelstam, CPL, 65.

this essay, Mandelstam delivered the speech in the Literary Society on April 25, 1914[30]):

> The Middle Ages are very close to us because they possessed to an extraordinary degree a sense of boundary and partitions. They never confused different levels and treated the beyond with the utmost restraint. A noble mixture of rationality and mysticism as well as a feeling for the world as a living equilibrium makes us kin to this epoch and encourages us to derive strength from the works that arose on Romance soil around the year 1200.[31]

This thought almost exactly coincides with what Pound wrote in the chapter "Il Miglior Fabbro," dedicated to Arnaut Daniel: "The twelfth century, or, more exactly, that century whose center is the year 1200, has left two perfect gifts: the church of San Zeno in Verona, and the canzoni of Arnaut Daniel; by which I would implicate all that is most excellent in the Italian-Romanesque architecture and in Provençal minstrelsy."[32] Pound started with *The Spirit of Romance* and for the rest of his life was faithful to "the spirit, which arose on Romance soil around the year 1200."[33] Beyond the features that Mandelstam, Pound, and T. S. Eliot have in common, as observed by Cavanagh in her book on Mandelstam discussed below,[34] the affinity of their ideas is due to the affinity of their sources. Homer, Dante, and Villon were more contemporary and real for Mandelstam, who translated the *Song of Roland* into Russian and, like Pound, wrote poems and essays dedicated to Hellenism and Medievalism, than the works of the Symbolists. In his essay "Nature of Word" (1921–1922), Mandelstam opposes Hellenism to Symbolism, revealing his attitude toward reality:

> Hellenism is the conscious surrounding of man with domestic utensils instead of impersonal objects; the transformation of impersonal objects into domestic utensils, and the humanizing and warming of the

---

30   See Osip Mandel'shtam, *Polnoe sobranie sochinenii i pisem*, comp. and ed. A. G. Mets (Moscow: Progress and Pleiada, 2010), vol. 2, 483.

31   CPL, 66.

32   Pound, *The Spirit of Romance*, 22.

33   Ibid.

34   Cf. Clare Cavanagh, *Osip Mandelstam and the Modernist Creation of Tradition* (Princeton, NJ: Princeton UP, 1995), 22.

surrounding world with the most delicate teleological warmth. [. . .] In the Hellenistic sense, symbols are domestic utensils, but then any object brought into man's sacred circle could become a utensil and consequently, a symbol.[35]

Mandelstam argues, "There is essentially no difference between a word and an image. An image is merely a word that has been sealed up and cannot be touched. An image is inappropriate for everyday use, just as an icon lamp would be inappropriate for lighting a cigarette." Then, by applying his views on the nature of a symbol to the school of Russian Symbolism that he called "pseudo-Symbolism," Mandelstam concludes,

> Jourdain discovered in his old age that he had been speaking "prose" all his life. The Russian Symbolists discovered the same prose, the primordial, image-bearing nature of the word. They sealed up all words, all images, designating them exclusively for liturgical use. An extremely awkward situation resulted: no one could move, nor stand up, nor sit down. One could no longer eat at table because it was no longer simply a table. One could no longer light a lamp because it might signify unhappiness later.[36]

Pound in "Vorticism" attacked Symbolism in a very similar fashion:

> The symbolists dealt in "association," that is, in a sort of allusion, almost an allegory. They degraded the symbol to the status of a word. They made it a form of metonymy. One can be grossly "symbolic," for example, by using the term "cross" to mean "trial." The symbolist's symbols have a fixed value, like numbers in arithmetic like 1, 2, and 7. The imagiste's images have a variable significance, like the signs a, b, and x in algebra.[37]

Both Pound in his essay of 1914 and Mandelstam in "The Morning of Acmeism" (1914) compare poetry to mathematics. Mandelstam puts it thus: "The sight of a mathematician who produces without effort the square of some ten-digit phenomenon to the tenth power, and the modest appearance of a work of art frequently deceives us with respect to the *monstrously condensed*

---

35   Mandelstam, CPL, 127–128.

36   Ibid., 128–129.

37   Ezra Pound, *Gaudier-Brzeska. A Memoir* (New York: New Directions, 1970), 84.

reality which it possesses."[38] Hence, both Mandelstam and Pound "overcame symbolism," to quote the 1916 essay by Victor Zhirmunskii dedicated to the early work of Gumilev, Akhmatova, and Mandelstam and bearing the same title.[39]

Gregory Freidin states that "in turn-of-the-century Europe, intensity in association with the paradigmatic (or, as in Mandelstam, the 'condensed reality' of a mathematical formula) denoted a phenomenon commanding the sort of reverence and respect afforded hidden springs of a tremendous power."[40] However, Mandelstam would later go farther and claim that "poetry is not a part of nature" and that it creates a different reality. In his essay "Vypad" [The slump], he argues that poetry "is not obliged to anyone, perhaps its creditors are all fraudulent!"[41] In the "Conversation About Dante," he states that "poetry is not a part of nature, not even its best or choicest part, let alone the reflection of it—this would make a mockery of the axioms of identity; rather, poetry establishes itself with astonishing independence in *a new extraspatial field of action*, not so much narrating as acting out in nature by means of its *arsenal of devices, commonly known as tropes*" (emphasis added).[42] Similarly, Pound emphasized the importance of image, stating, "The image is the poet's pigment. The painter should use his colour because he sees it or feels it. I don't much care whether he is representative or non-representative. He should depend, of course, on the creative, not upon the mimetic or representational part in his work."[43]

Furthermore, there is a striking affinity in both Mandelstam's and Pound's views on the nature of poetry. In the "Conversation about Dante," Mandelstam asserts:

> It is only with the severest qualifications that poetic discourse or thought may be referred to as "sounding"; for we hear in it only the crossing of two lines, one of which, taken by itself, is completely mute,

---

38 Mandelstam, CPL, 61 (emphasis added).

39 Viktor Zhirmunskii, "Preodolevshie simvolizm," in *Poetika russkoi poezii* (St. Petersburg: Azbuka-klassika, 2001), 364–404.

40 Gregory Freidin, *A Coat of Many Colors. Osip Mandelstam and His Mythologies of Self-Presentation* (Los Angeles and Berkeley, CA: California UP, 1985), 12.

41 Mandelstam, CPL, 202.

42 Ibid., 397 (emphasis added).

43 Pound, Gaudier-Brzeska, 86.

while the other, abstracted from its prosodic transmutation, is totally devoid of significance and interest, and is susceptible of paraphrasing, which, to my mind, is surely a sign of non-poetry. For where there is amenability to paraphrase, there the sheets have never been rumpled, there poetry, so to speak, has never spent the night.[44]

In *ABC of Reading*, Pound maintains, very much like Mandelstam, that "music rots when it gets too far from the dance. Poetry atrophies when it gets too far from music."[45] Hence, for Pound and Mandelstam the nature of poetry is inseparable from music, the understanding of which goes far beyond meter and rhythm for both poets.

Both Pound and Mandelstam were concerned with the renewal of literature, especially of the language of poetry, but both considered Futurism a narrow-minded escape from the past and from tradition. As Pound said in "Vorticisim," defying Marinetti, "We do not desire to evade comparison with the past. We prefer that the comparison be made by some intelligent person whose idea of 'the tradition' is not limited by the conventional taste of four or five centuries and one continent."[46] In "The Morning of Acmeism" Mandelstam also opposes Futurism, aiming primarily at Mayakovsky:

> [T]he Futurists, unable to cope with conscious sense as creative material, frivolously threw it overboard and essentially repeated the crude mistake of their predecessors. For the Acmeists, the conscious sense of the word, Logos, is just as magnificent a form as music is for the Symbolists. And if, for the Futurists, the word as such is still down on its knees creeping, in Acmeism it has for the first time assumed a dignified upright position and entered the Stone Age of its existence.[47]

Pound would also be the last modernist to defy Logos, since he managed to express the same idea in an aphoristic form: "Great Literature is simply language charged with meaning to the utmost possible degree."[48]

Thus, both Mandelstam and Pound were opposed to Symbolism, Futurism, and mimesis. Mandelstam's understanding of reality was probably closer

---

44   Mandelstam, CPL, 397.

45   Ezra Pound, *ABC of Reading* (New York: New Directions, 1987), 61 (hereafter ABC).

46   Pound, *Gaudier-Brzeska*, 90.

47   Mandelstam, CPL, 62.

48   Pound, *ABC*, 36.

to that of Ortega y Gasset, who believed that there are as many realities as points of view (so-called "perspectivism"). Mandelstam's reality is always a condensed image. Sometimes his reality is close to Impressionism:

> The artist painted
> How deeply lilacs fainted,
> Ply over ply, resounding colors
> He dabbed like scabs on canvas.

The poem was most probably inspired by Claude Monet's painting *"Lilacs in the Sun"* (1873), which is now in the Pushkin Fine Arts Museum in Moscow that was founded by Ivan Vladimirovich Tsvetaev (1847–1913), Marina Tsvetaeva's father.[49] The painting was included in the exposition in the Museum of New Western Art in 1932 attended by Mandelstam and his wife. Perhaps Mandelstam, a great lover of Impressionism, was acquainted with modern painting during his studies in Paris in 1907–1908, as was pointed out by Irina Surat.[50] That makes sense since there is no bumblebee in the picture, and the poet might have brought his own experience from his visit to France when he added:

> A shade grows more violet with each touch!
> A whistle or a whip dies like a match.
> You'll say: chefs in the kitchens
> Are cooking now fat pigeons.

Evidently, there is nothing like that in the picture, and it was most probably in France, not in Russia (let alone in the 1930s), where chefs were "cooking fat pigeons" for dinner.

Mandelstam's peculiar play of associations can bring together disjointed images. For example, his poem "Venetian Life" ("The meaning of fruitless and gloomy /Venetian life to me is light") combines references to at least two paintings by a Venetian artist.[51] The first painting is a portrait of a Venetian lady:

---

49   Claude Monet's painting "Lilacs in the Sun" can be found here: https://www.wikiart.org/fr/claude-monet/lilas-au-soleil-1872.

50   Irina Surat, "On Osip Mandelstam's Poem 'Impressionism,'" *Studia Literaturum* 6, no. 3 (2021): 170.

51   As suggested by Alexander Kulik in "'Znacheniie svetlo': kliuch k 'Venitseiskoi zhizni' Osipa Mandel'shtama" [The meaning is light: key to "Venetian life" by Osip Mandelstam].

> The meaning of fruitless and gloomy
> Venetian life to me is bright.
> Here she looks smiling coolly
> In the old blue glass' sight.

In the draft copy, the following stanza read: "Thin air, skin's delicate veins," as mentioned in the commentary of the Mets edition.[52] Therefore, it is skin, not leather; moreover, "white snow" is a metaphor of the lady's skin and "green brocade" refers to "heavy attires," as seen in both paintings of Titian.[53]

Besides Mandelstam's ekphrastic imagination, there is an idea of human doom and mortality:

> The candles keep burning, burning in the baskets
> As if the dove flew back into the Ark.
> At the theater and at the assembly banquets
> Man dies in light or in dark.

Hence, "Everyone is put onto a cypress [funeral] bier," not in sedan chairs, as one translator put it, especially if we recollect another Mandelstam's poem from *Tristia* (1920): "Man dies, and hot sand is cooling down, /And a black bier carries away yesterday's sun."

> Blue veins. Skin's delicate air.
> White snow. Green brocade's yoke.
> Everyone is put onto a cypress bier,
> Sleepy and warm, plucked out from one's cloak.

Green brocade and a snow-white skin are seen in both Titian's *Woman with a Mirror* (1515) and Vanity (ca 1520), while the second painting as suggested by Kulik, might be *Susana and the Elders* by Tintoreḋo from the Vienna, which follows the Biblical plot of Susanna and the Elders, from the Book of Daniel (see note 51):

Wiener Slavistiches Jahrbuch 3 (2015): 108-109, Osip Mandelstam might refer to the painting by Bernardo Strozzi Vanitas [Old Coquette] (c. 1637), now in the collection of Pushkin State Museum while *Susanna and the Elders* might refer to the painting of Tintoretto from the Vienna Art Museum.

52   Mandel'shtam, *Polnoe sobranie sochinenii i pisem*, 1:568.

53   See for instance, *Vanity* (ca 1520) and *Woman with a Mirror* (ca 1515; holding a phial or a flask) Cf.: Gasparov, Mikhail and Omri Ronen "O 'Venitseiskoi zhizni' O. Mandel'shtama". *Zvezda* 2, 2002: 193-2002, esp. 196, 201.

> Black Vesper flickers in the mirror glass.
> Everything passes. Dark truth bewilders.
> A man is born. A pearl dies, alas.
> And Susanna has to wait for the Elders.

Sometimes Mandelstam's reality is closer to Surrealism:

> So play to the rapture of aorta
> With a cat's head in your mouth,
> There were three devils, you're the fourth,
> The last, marvelous colorful sprite.[54]
> (*April 5–July 1935*)

If we do not seek literal likeness, we could probably grasp the image-pictures (or soundscape in Marjorie Perloff's dictum)[55] of this poem: "the rapture of aorta" is the fate of the artist; "the cat's head in your mouth" is the sound image inspired by the performance of a lady-violinist (Galina Barinova, according to Nadezhda Mandelstam's "Commentaries"[56]), "the devils" were, perhaps, Paganini, Veniavsky, and Fritz Kreisler. According to Aleksandr Mets, who diligently compared all the drafts of this as well as of many other poems by Mandelstam, this stanza was in the beginning of the very first draft, and by "the gypsy crowd" the poet meant violinists.[57] Then, in his usual manner, Mandelstam hid allusions and moved the first stanza to the end of the poem.

In Mandelstam's poems, the image of time itself is sometimes "hidden" and must be decoded:

> After midnight the heart feasts,
> Having bitten a silvery mouse.

According to Nadezhda Mandelstam, the "silvery mouse" is an image of time, which, probably, was inspired by Maximilan Voloshin and Greek philosophy,

---

54 The translation is mine.

55 Marjorie Perloff coined this word to described Velimir Khlebnikov's treatment of the word. See Marjorie Perloff, *21ˢᵗ-Century Modernism: The "New" Poetics* (Oxford: Blackwell, 2002), 121.

56 Cf. Nadezhda Mandel'shtam, "Kommentarii," 258.

57 Aleksandr Mets, *Osip Mandel'shtam i ego vremia: Analiz tekstov* (St. Petersburg: n. p., 2011), 169.

as she wrote in *The Second Book* and her *Commentary*. She also mentioned Indian philosophy but was not sure if Osip Mandelstam knew it.[58]

Still, in his dealings with time, Mandelstam was a contemporary concerned with life and the present: "Just try and rip me out of the time!— // You'll wring your own neck, I'm telling you!"[59] His thirst for reality was almost as great as his thirst for world culture. Although his approach to reality and time was often hostile, his attitude was far from straightforward.

The most vivid example of Mandelstam's complex approach to art and reality is revealed in his visionary poem "Verses on the Unknown Soldier" that evokes his vision of the past, present, and future of humankind based on history and science.

Mandelstam persistently followed the scientific inventions of his time. He was aware that science could bring destruction and chaos, as he predicted in "Verses on The Unknown Soldier" (1937), as did Pound in Canto 115. The poem "Verses on The Unknown Soldier" begins with a vision of a human ocean that lacks sight and foresight ("Let this air be called a witness: / The long-ranged heart that it has, and in dug-outs, omnivorous and active / Is the ocean, windowless stuff . . ."),[60] and then reveals a cosmic vision:

> Through the ether of ten-digit zeroes
> The light of speeds ground down to a beam
> Starts a number, made lucent and clear
> By the bright pain of holes and moles.
>
> And beyond the field of fields a new battlefield
> Flies like a triangular flock of cranes,
> The news flies like a new dust-like light,
> And it's bright from the yesterday's fight.
>
> The news flies like a new light-dust:
> —I am not Leipzig, not Waterloo,
> Not the Battle of Nations—I am new,
> I will dazzle the world with my light.

---

58   Nadezhda Mandelstam, "Kommentarii," 199.

59   Osip Mandelstam, *The Complete Poetry of Osip Mandelstam*, trans. Burton Raffel and Anna Burago (Albany, NY: State University of New York Press, 1973).

60   Bernard Meares's translation; for my translation, see p. 257.

Arabian mess, mash and hash,
The light of speeds ground down to a ray—
And trampling my retina with its squint soles,
The beam flattens the apple of my eye.[61]

Mandelstam's vision here recalls Yeats's "Second Coming" and Pound's "Hell Cantos." The Russian poet's vision differs from that of Yeats, however, since it is revealed in an incredible blend of scientific images and vocabulary and, at the same time, genuine metaphors. Though Mandelstam begins with the hell of past wars, the lines quoted above alluding to World War I, his "Soldier" also differs from Pound's "Hell Cantos" because Mandelstam expresses a cosmic vision and goes far beyond particulars. Yuri Levin maintains that Mandelstam's entire poem is set by Block's line "A horrid sight of future wars" and evokes "a complex image of a global war."[62] V. V. Ivanov presumes that this poem reflects the old scientific theories, such as that of ether, as well as the newest, in particular the velocity of the speed of light ($C=300,000$ km/sec) and Einstein's theory of relativity and the formula $E=MC^2$ that eventually led to the invention of the nuclear bomb.[63] Levin lists its main themes: Cosmos and Nature, War and Death.

Mandelstam is perhaps the most intricate Russian poet of the twentieth century, known for his esoteric and complex allusions and associations mostly hidden between the lines. Mandelstam's reader, like the reader of Yeats and Pound, has to do a lot of research in order to decode his texts. As for allusions and associations, Nadezhda Mandelstam as well as the scholars mentioned above point out Ezekiel, Shakespeare's *Hamlet*, the poetry of Lomonosov, Derzhavin, Baratynsky's "Skull" [Cherep], Lermontov's "Demon," Zedlitz's "Die Nächtliche Heerschau" [The night parade] in Zhukovsky's translation, and Flammarion. In addition, Mikhail Gasparov mentions Erich Remarque's novel *All Quiet on the Western Front* (1929), Henri Barbusse's *Fire*, as well as the Russian writer Vladimir Lidin's novel *The Grave of the Unknown Soldier* and Arcady Shteinberg's (1907–1984) expressionist poem of 1933 bearing the same title.

---

61 Translation is mine.

62 Iurii Levin, "Zametki o poezii Mandel'shtama 30-kh godov. II. "Stikhi o neizvestnom soldate," *Slavica Hierosolymitana* 4 (1979): 185–212.

63 Viacheslav V. Ivanov, "'Stikhi o neizvestnom soldate' v kontekste mirovoi poesii," in *Zhizn' i tvorchestvo O. E. Mandel'shtama* (Voronezh: Voronezhskii gosudarstvennyi universitet, 1990), 360.

Gasparov proves that Shteinberg's poem alludes to Lermontov's "Napoleon" and Zedlitz's "Die Nächtliche Heerschau," and shows that it deals with themes of darkness and future eternal light, purgatory and resurrection.[64] The poems of German poet Max Bartel "To the Unknown Soldier" and "Verdun," which Mandelstam himself translated into Russian in the middle of 1920s, can certainly be added to that list. In addition, there is a certain affinity between the opening of Mandelstam's "Soldier" and Apollinaire's surrealist poem "Ocean of Earth" dedicated to G. de Chirico and translated into Russian by Benedict Livshits, an acquaintance of Mandelstam, a prominent translator of French poetry and a superb poet close to the Futurists, also a victim of Stalin's purges, who was shot on September 21, 1938, as an "enemy of the people" accused of "Trotsky conspiracy." In particular, the fragment below bears a striking resemblance to the spirit of Mandelstam's "Soldier":

> Airplanes drop eggs
> Watch out for the anchor
> Watch out for the ink which they squirt
> It's a good thing you came from the sky
> The honeysuckle of the sky climbs up
> The earthly octopus throb
> And then we are closer and closer to being our own grave-diggers
> Pale octopus of chalky waves O octopus with pale beaks
> Around the house there is this ocean which you know
> And which is never still.[65]

The vision of Mandelstam's poem, however, goes beyond all scientific and literary allusions and shows such a state of humanity, in which light itself becomes darkness.

---

64 Semën Lipkin, "Vtoraia doroga," in *K verkhov'iam*, by Arkadii Shteinberg (Moscow: Sovpadeniie, 1997), 361. Lipkin proved that another poem of Shteinberg, "Wolf Hunting," attracted the attention of both Mayakovsky and Mandelstam, who wrote his famous poem "For the thunderous courage of ages to come" alluding to certain metaphors in Shteinberg's text. Therefore, it is most likely that in his "Verses on The Unknown Soldier," Mandelstam also alluded to the poem of his younger contemporary, who would later share the great poet's fate of spending more than ten years in Stalin's camps and then would become one of the greatest Russian translators of poetry, in particular, the best translator of Milton's *Paradise Lost*.

65 *Modern European Poetry*, trans. Roger Shattuck and Willis Barnstone (Toronto, New York, and London: Bantam Books, 1966), 9–10.

Mandelstam's "light" differs of course from that of Pound's "Nous," the Neoplatonic light of his *The Cantos*. At the end of the poem, written mostly in the third person, Mandelstam shifts to the first person singular to "dissolve in humanity":

> Aortas are flooded with blood,
> And a whisper spreads through the ranks:
>   —"I was born in the year ninety-four,
>   —I was born in the year ninety-two . . ."
> And squeezing in my fist a worn date of birth,
> With bloodless lips I whisper amid crowd and herd:
> "I was born on the night from the second to the third
> Of January in the unreliable year
> Of ninety-one, and centuries
> Encircle me with fire."
> *(March 1–15, 1937)*

The end of the poem not only symbolizes Mandelstam's reunion with humankind on the eve of annihilation and his vision of the Last Judgement, but also seems like a prediction of his own horrible fate, when, "squashing" a number in his fist, deprived of his name and personality, the poet will be dissolved in the multitudes of persecuted exiles thrown into Stalin's camps. Although M. L. Gasparov correctly stated that at the end of the poem Mandelstam showed soldiers drafted into the army, not prisoners of the Soviet concentration camps in the Gulag, since they are calling out the year of their birth, not prisoners' numbers,[66] Mandelstam never served in the army, but he did serve his first prison term in Cherdyn', Perm oblast, in the Urals, in 1934–1935 until he was pardoned and exiled to Voronezh. Nevertheless, Mandelstam's vision is more terrifying than Dante's hell, since even the worst sinners in the *Inferno* preserve their names and personalities. However, in another poem of 1937 (written the same year as the "Verses of the Unknown Soldier"), Mandelstam says that the sky of purgatory is temporary, though we forget that in our suffering, "This happy heaven's depot / Is our expending and lifetime homestead." Thus, Mandelstam fearlessly faces reality and, like Pound, claims that paradise is here on earth.

Yeats, Mandelstam, and Pound were seeking the renewal of language, poetry, and art by "charging the language with meaning to the utmost degree"

---

66   Gasparov, *Grazhdanskaia lirika Mandel'shtama*, 14–15.

and conveying their vision in images. Though they were all seeking reality, they did not do so in a literal way; for them reality was, first and foremost, spiritual. Therefore, one of the main sources of the renewal they sought was the birthplace of civilization: Hellas, the Mediterranean, and, more characteristic for Mandelstam and for Pound, Medievalism. Unlike Yeats, neither Mandelstam nor Pound ever attempted to escape reality and the present. Nor did they seek "the artifice of eternity." As stated above, Mandelstam and Pound did not see a contradiction between nature, reality and eternity, and each was trying to create his "earthly paradise" in his own way. Both Mandelstam and Pound had a similar attitude toward nature "as a system of powers immanent in organic life forms and even in inorganic matter," human nature, nature as "a play of physical and chemical processes"[67] as well as toward the natural sciences and scientific language. Both sought ways to overcome Symbolism and Futurism, and they had the same approach to mimesis. Although they never read a line of each other's writing, the affinities between Mandelstam and Pound were due to the affinities of their sources—Hellenism, High Antiquity, Medievalism, Dante, and Villon.

One of such meaningful points of intersection for them all was Byzantium. Yeats wrote in his diary that if he could have lived a month in the time of high antiquity, he would have chosen Byzantium some time before Justinian built the church of St. Sophia and closed Plato's Academy. The protagonist of his poem "Sailing to Byzantium" has chosen exactly this time and space. Unlike Yeats, Pound meticulously draws the City's history, focusing on the right to coin money, *The Eparch's Book* of Leo the Wise (886–911), Del Mar's writings, social credit theory ("and of course there is no local freedom / without local control of purchasing power"), and carefully avoids fancy symbols and high-flown poetic language. However, by making the construction of St. Sophia the climax of Canto 96 (reinforced in Canto 97), he creates precisely that which he has been trying to escape or at least not to say out loud: a monument "of unageing intellect." As Ronald Bush observed,

> An aestheticized image of Byzantium very close to the one memorialized by Yeats animates both the subject and the treatment of *Thrones.* For however much Pound believes himself to be creating an ideogram of wise leadership, only with difficulty can one glean from his texts the

---

67 Burton Hatlen, "Pound and Nature: Reading of Canto XXIII," *Paideuma* 25, nos. 1–2 (Spring–Fall 1996): 163.

clear outlines of legal and administrative policy. These Cantos concern themselves not with the ordinary life of society but with gem-like clarity of an idealized moment when the whole of culture has become a work of art.[68]

Moreover, rhyming ideas and images, Pound places St. Sophia beside the Malatesta Tempio (or rather vice versa), admiring both creators, Sigismondo, the protagonist of Cantos 8–11, and Justinian, the protagonist of Canto 96 and later cantos, including *Thrones. Templum aedeficavit* [built the temple] in Canto 90/605, as a hymn to the creator, corresponds to Pound's citation of Horace in his eulogy for Yeats: "A great peacock aere perennius" in Canto 83/534. Therefore, Byzantium can be viewed as a symbol of cultural heritage and civilization both for Yeats and Pound, while the church of St. Sophia is, for Pound, a symbol and gem of Byzantium, even though he was preoccupied with Dionysian, not Christian, mysteries. As Wilhelm observed, Pound "saw the great cathedral rising out of the hubbub, just as he himself envisioned the formation of the canto."[69]

The church of St. Sophia ("Hagia Sophia") appears twice in Osip Mandelstam's poetry: in "The Octaves" and in his early poem of 1912:

> Hagia Sophia—it was commanded by the Lord
> That here kings and nations halt amazed!
> Your cupola, in the eyewitness' word,
> As if towards heaven on a chain was raised. [70]

As Hansen-Löve maintains, "In contrast to the Symbolist myth of the city and parallel to the Futurist urbanism and love of technology, the Acmeist world city has its own geography and conception of history. In the foreground is the historically established culture of the city, the archetype of the polis as the abode of culture in which urbis and orbis coincide."[71]

---

68   Ronald Bush, "Late Cantos LXXII–CXVII," in *The Cambridge Companion to Ezra Pound*, ed. Ira B. Nadel (Cambridge: Cambridge University Press, 1999), 123.

69   J. J. Wilhelm, *The Later Cantos of Ezra Pound* (New York: Walker, 1977), 132.

70   Translations, if not otherwise mentioned, are mine.

71   Aage Hansen-Löve, "Mandel'shtam's Thanatopoetics," in *Readings in Russian Modernism. To Honor Vladimir Fedorovich Markov*, ed. Ronald Vroon and John Malmstad (Los Angeles, CA: U of California P, 1993), 125.

Mandelstam never visited Constantinople, but he read Dmitry Ainalov's book *The Hellenistic Foundations of Byzantine Art* (1900) and in 1912 attended his lectures on the history of architecture in the auditorium of the Museum of Ancient History (a great deal of those lectures was dedicated to Hagia Sophia and the Cathedral of Notre Dame in Paris), as mentioned by Przybylski.[72] The eyewitness to the construction of Hagia Sophia, as Przybylski noted, was Procopius of Caesaria, the philosopher of history known for his *Secret History*. Procopius described the enormous cupola of the basilica as so light that it seemed to be suspended "miraculously from heaven on a golden chain and hung above the earth."[73] Cavanagh argues that Hagia Sophia, "suspended on a chain from heaven, itself becomes a lamp hanging from an infinitely vaster ceiling."[74] I would, however, agree with Przybylski that the movement in Mandelstam's poem is the opposite: the cupola is evidently raised towards heaven by humans, not by God. Likewise, in Canto 96 Pound emphasizes the process of the construction of the temple, which was actually the third structure built in 537 AD, "unlikely to fall," after the two previous buildings had been destroyed by fire: "After all Justinian's boy had built Santa Sophia" (C. 96/662).

Mandelstam views the temple from a slightly different vantage point:

> Justinian has set a pattern for all ages
> When Diana of Ephesus as a marvel
> Allowed him to abduct for alien gods
> One hundred seven verdant pillars made of marble.

The Ephesian Diana "allowed" Justinian to abduct or to steal [in Russian, *pokhitit'*] 107 green marble pillars from her temple, Artemision, one of the nine wonders of the world, as observed by Przybylski.[75] Thus, in Mandelstam's view, Diana was blessing the new temple of Divine Wisdom and the new religion, Christianity, which was the real cause of the temple's firmness, not just its solid foundation. Although not exactly like Pound, Mandelstam connects paganism and Christianity, or rather, he emphasizes the continuity of human history and civilization. As Przybylski states, "The history of humanity is an uninterrupted procession of generations, nations and kings. The Church

---

72   Przybylski, *An Essay on the Poetry of Osip Mandelstam*, 108.

73   Ibid., 109.

74   Cavanagh, *Osip Mandelstam and the Modernist Creation*, 74.

75   Przybylski, *An Essay on the Poetry of Osip Mandelstam*, 110.

of Divine Wisdom is the place in which God stopped the flow of history. To use the poet's own words, this church is 'a cross-section of time,' an organism, a system, thanks to which history acquires meaning."[76]

Przybylski then points out that "the place designated for stopping" was unusual, since "Constantinople was originally a copy of pagan Rome. As in Rome all the streets, all traffic led to the center, where the temple of Jupiter was located. Hagia Sophia was erected on that spot. It is a sort of second Hellenic Center of Existence, if only because Constantinople was the second Rome."[77] Moreover, Mandelstam binds together East and West, united by divine wisdom, Sophia:

> But what was thinking your generous builder
> When elevated both in mind and spirit
> He set out your apses and exedrae to bewilder
> Pointing them towards West and East?

The Russian philosopher Konstantin Leontiev (1831–1891) wrote in his work *Byzantinism and Slavism* (1875) that the Western Christian world acquired its culture, spirit, law, and religion from the Western Roman empire and then during the Renaissance, which Leontiev called "the epoch of complexity blossoming as the result of late contact with Roman-Germanic and Byzantine cultures," while the Eastern Slavic world acquired both its religion and culture directly from Byzantium.[78] Although Mandelstam disliked both Leontiev and the idea of Byzantinism, as Przybylski correctly noted, quoting Mandelstam's "The Noise of Time,"[79] the idea expressed in "Hagia Sophia" goes far beyond Byzantinism and Pan-Slavism in a Leontievian sense. Mandelstam emphasizes the continuity (*Sagetrieb*, in Pound's dictum) of human civilization and spirit. Hence, the beautiful edifice is a celebration of light and as such will outlive nations, kings, and ages.[80]

---

76   Ibid., 109.

77   Ibid.

78   Konstantin Leont'ev, "Vizantism i slavianstvo," in *Vostok, Rossiia, Slavianstvo* (Moscow: Respublika, 1996), 95. Translation is mine.

79   See Przybylski, *An Essay on the Poetry of Osip Mandelstam*, 107.

80   Thus, this poem can be also considered the response of the young Mandelstam to Derzhavin's "River of Time" and the theme of oblivion (discussed below).

> Beautiful is the temple bathing in the world,
> And its forty windows are the triumph of light,
> But the most beautiful of all are the four gold
> Archangels on the pendentives on high.
>
> And the wise spherical building
> Will last through ages and nations will outlive,
> And even seraphim's resonant weeping
> Will not distort the dark gold leaf.

Unlike Mandelstam, Yeats does not feel the harmony between the divine wisdom as represented by St. Sophia and "the fury and the mire of human veins":

> A starlit or a moonlit dome disdains
> All that man is,
> All mere complexities,
> The fury and the mire of human veins.
> *("Byzantium," 1932)*

Pound, on the other hand, seems to combine both approaches, drawing heavily on the history of Byzantium, the battles and laws of Justinian and Leo the Wise's edicts, but he utters in the middle of it: "'Constantinople' said Wyndham 'our star,' / Mr. Yeats called it Byzantium" (C. 96/681).

Thus, Byzantium is the place where the two civilizations and cultures meet, and this thought sheds light on the similarity of Mandelstam's, Yeats's, and Pound's philosophical ideas and themes. All three seek to reunite time, culture and spirit, or perhaps to find such a point of observation in the universe from which time, history, and civilization can be seen in their entirety. Therefore, the main theme of *Thrones*, subtly explicated by Massimo Bacigalupo, can be considered the theme of *The Cantos* as a whole: "Kings and cultures appear united in a timeless renaissance of civilization, intimately connected with the only valid model of rebirth: the new frond, the instant 'gone as lightning,' yet, 'enduring 5000 years (c. 95).'"[81]

In their courageous attempt to reunite time and civilization, the poets, through their lyrical heroes, depart from the present and sail through the ages. Sea voyage or wandering is both the medium and the metaphor for all three

---

81   Massimo Bacigalupo, *The Forméd Trace: The Later Poetry of Ezra Pound* (New York: Columbia UP, 1980), 367.

poets under consideration. To this end, Yeats uses his own lyrical hero, while Pound and Mandelstam employ the persona of either Odysseus or the Seafarer, as in Pound's translation of the eighth-century Anglo-Saxon text and in Mandelstam's "Nashedhii podkovu" [The Horseshoe Finder, 1923]. In Mandelstam's poem, an "unbridled passion for space," a desire to sail "beyond the Gates of Hercules" erases the boundary between time and space:

> And the seafarer,
> In his untamed thirst for space
> Drags through soggy furrows
> The fragile instrument of a geometer,
> To weigh the rugged surface of the seas
> Against the attraction of the terrestrial bosom.[82]

Mandelstam's seafarer may be Odysseus (since he is called "the father of seafarers, the friend of the seafarer"), but Steven Broyde and Cavanagh do not exclude Peter the Great, since he was also a shipbuilder, though not "Bethlehem's peaceful carpenter." Moreover, alluding to Mandelstam's earlier poem of 1918 "Proslavim, brat'ya sumerki svobody" [Hail, brothers, let us praise our freedom's twilight], Cavanagh even supposes that Mandelstam's "father of a seafarer" might be Lenin himself, which is more than doubtful in my view.[83]

As mentioned by a number of scholars, the rhythm and imagery of Mandelstam's poem allude to Pindar. Broyde points out the Seventh Nemean (15) and the Third Pythian Odes (89–90) of Pindar as the source of Mandelstam's verses, as well as Hesiod's *Theogony* (915–917), in which the Muses and their mother Mnemosyne are crowned with frontlets.[84] I. Kovaleva adds The Fourth Isthmian and the Third Nemean Odes of Pindar.[85] Cavanagh also mentions Pindar's Sixth and Ninth Olympian Odes, the Fifth Nemean Ode, and the Eleventh Pythian Ode;[86] and Broyde supposes the influence

---

82   Translation is mine.

83   Cf. Cavanagh, *Osip Mandelstam and the Modernist Creation*, 168.

84   See S. J. Broyde, "Osip Mandelstam's 'Nasedsij Podkovu,'" *Slavic Poetics. Essays in Honor of Kiril Taranovsky* (Paris: Mouton, 1973), 49–66.

85   Irina Kovaleva and Anton Nesterov, "Pindar i Mandel'shtam (K postanovke problemy)," in *Mandel'shtam i antichnost'* (Moscow: Rossiiskii gosudarstvennyi gumanitarnyi universitet, 1995), 166–168.

86   See Cavanagh, Osip Mandelstam and the Modernist Creation, 172–173, 183.

of Ovid's *Amores* (II, II, 1–4).[87] In addition, Kovaleva suggests the beginning of Catullus's Ode LXIV.[88]

It is true that Mandelstam juxtaposes the successful Pindar with his own fate as a literary and cultural outcast in the Soviet state. According to Cavanagh, "The Horseshoe Finder" is "a poem about failure, both personal and artistic."[89] I would argue that the poem is not about artistic failure, since Mandelstam was well aware of his genius and was still a recognized and published author until the 1930s (the last book published during his lifetime, *Poems*, came out in 1928). As for his personal failure, it was a conscious choice announced in "January 1, 1924":

> Can I betray to a shameful smear—
> The frost smells of apple again—
> The wonderful oath to the fourth estate
> And the wows as great as tears?[90]

Mandelstam nonetheless looked far beyond the present to overcome the fear of persecution, arrest, execution, and oblivion by "combining the uncombinable" through "a synchronism of events, names, and traditions severed by centuries," as Mandelstam wrote in his "Razgovor o Dante" [Conversation about Dante].[91] Yet, time is not only a fearful giant but also "a sick beast" for Mandelstam. In "Vek" [The age, 1922], he refers to time as to "a sick and dying

---

87   See Broyde, "Osip Mandelstam's 'Naseddsij Podkovu,'" 49–66.

88   Kovaleva and Nesterov, "Pindar i Mandel'shtam," 166—168.

89   Cavanagh, Osip Mandelstam and the Modernist Creation, 158.

90   Unlike the contemporary notion of the "fourth estate" as journalists and free press, historically, since the 1840s, it was used to denote proletariat. The term is attributed to the German journalist and political writer Rudolf Hermann Meyer (Friedeberg, Neumark, 1839–Dessau, 1899) who first used it in his work *Emanzipationskampf des vierten Standes* [Liberation of the fourth estate, 1874–1875]. Hence, the stanza reveals Mandelstam's spiritual struggle between the "pledge" to the liberation of the proletariat and the actual terror in the name of the proletariat he was witnessing. The "pledge" may also allude to the oath of the two Russian prominent thinkers and writers Alexander Herzen (1812–1870) and Nikolai Ogarëv (1813–1877) who in the summer of 1827, during a walk in the Sparrow Hills above Moscow, made an oath not to rest until their country was free; the oath reportedly sustained them and their friends throughout many crises of their lives at home and abroad and was described in E. H. Carr's (1892–1982) *The Romantic Exiles* (London: Victor Gollancz, 1933).

91   Mandelstam, CPL, 420.

beast," while in "January 1 1924," age is portrayed as a dying tyrant who will nevertheless "sink onto the numb arm of an aging son."[92] "The era was ringing as a golden sphere," wrote Mandelstam in "The Horseshoe Finder," alluding to the Golden Age.[93] As Nadezhda Mandelstam recollected, the poet later called the nineteenth century "the Golden Age."[94]

In "January 1, 1924" Mandelstam opposes sick time to the roaring rivers of deceptive and desolate times, alluding both to bloody reality and to Derzhavin's (1743–1816) last unfinished poem "Reka vremën" [River of time]. Hence the necessity to heal or save sick time ("the time is out of joint," to quote Shakespeare), even at the cost of the poet's own life. Therefore, the theme of overcoming separation in time and isolation in civilization and culture by healing or saving time and beginning a new world was inevitably connected in Mandelstam's poetry with the theme of art:

> To tear the age from bounds,
> To found a new world,

---

92   As convincingly shown by Ronen, the theme of the aging (sick, weak) son of a sick (decrepit) age goes back to Lermontov, Gogol, Nekrasov (who uses the phrase "you are the sick son of a sick age" in his "Poet i grazhdanin" [Poet and citizen]), Grigoriev, Sologub ("I am also the sick son of a sick age"), Annensky ("I am the weak son of a sick generation"), and Blok; and to Chateaubriand's "mal du René" and Musset's "mal du siècle" (echoed by Alexander Herzen's (1812–1870) *S togo berega* [From the other shore]. Cf. Omry Ronen, *An Approach To Mandelstam* (Jerusalem: The Magness Press and the Hebrew University, 1983), 248–250.

93   Cavanagh correctly noticed that "The Horseshoe Finder" "abounds in images of circles and spheres, whether partial or full" (*Osip Mandelstam and the Modernist Creation*, 159). However, she also includes in that group the lintel or threshhold (*porog*) that is defined in Dal's *Dictionary of the Russian Language* as "a cross-cut height or elevation, something that blocks, an obstacle," which is certainly a plain, vertical object, especially in a Russian house; further, Cavanagh mentions a mysterious "green ball" from the line: "A rustle runs across the trees like a green ball," misread by the translator since the Russian word *lapta*, as defined by Dal's *Dictionary*, is "a flat thing, one end of which is wider than the other, a stick or a bat with which a ball is hit" in an old Russian game similar to baseball. In other words, the trees that are obviously seen as green spheres are hit with a stick or a bat. The line should be rendered as "a rustle runs through the trees hit by a green bat" or even as "a rustle runs through the green spheres of trees hit by a bat." Thus, Mandelstam opposes spheres to flat piercing objects, as he begins the poem by contrasting a plumbline to "dump furrows of the seas" and describes pines that "once stood on the earth uncomfortable as a mule's backbone." Therefore, the imagery of the poem is even subtler than perceived by Cavanagh whose book is otherwise solid and coherent.

94   Nadezhda Mandelstam, *Hope against Hope*, 271.

> The knotty joints of days
> Should be bound by flute sounds.
> (*The Age*)

Here "the flute is a metonymy of art, poetry," as Efim Etkind put it.[95] Similarly, in "The Horseshoe Finder," the theme of wandering and spiritual quest is connected with the art of poetry:

> Thrice-blesséd is he who puts a name in a song;
> A song embossed with a name
> Outlives the others—
> It is set apart from her girlfriends by a headband,
> Healing from oblivion by a befuddling odor too strong to endure—
> Whether caused by the imminence of a man
> Or the smell of a strong beast's fur,
> Or just by the scent of thyme grated by the palms.

In Mandelstam's poem, oblivion (or amnesia) is caused by an overly strong, befuddling smell, the source of which might be the closeness of a male, or the smell of a strong wild beast's hair, which corresponds to Yeats's vision:

> . . . The young
> In one another's arms, birds in the trees,
> Those dying generations—at their song,
> The salmon-falls, the mackerel-crowded seas,
> Fish, flesh, or fowl, commend all summer long
> Whatever is begotten, born and dies.
> Caught in that sensual music all neglect
> Monuments of unageing intellect.[96]

Yeats's "sensual music" of dying generations and Mandelstam's amnesia have the same causes, and the vital power of procreation can lead to unbeing if not saved by creativity or by the "monuments of unageing intellect."

At the outset, the Acmeists called themselves Adamists, declaring that a poet, like Biblical Adam, names things, thus bringing them back to life and preserving them in eternity. To name the phenomena of the world is to reveal them. Revelation is re-evaluation: re-veiling and unveiling something so

---

95   Etkind, "Osip Mandel'shtam—Trilogiia o veke," 260.

96   Yeats, "Sailing to Byzantium," in *The Collected Poems of W. B. Yeats*, ed. Richard J. Finneran (New York: Collier Books and Macmillan, 1989), 193.

palpable and fragile that when "rendered in disdainful prose," as Pushkin said, it evaporates. Having acquired a name, the object acquires being and is saved from oblivion. Therefore, language is an instrument of the comprehension of being, and naming, as one of the functions of poetry, is connected to the comprehension of time, space, and being as a whole. Levin mentioned that all the poems of Mandelstam's "Crimean-Hellenic" cycle have "a feeling of the integrity of time and space."[97]

However, the search to unite time that is "out of joint" is both a dangerous quest and difficult work for the poet. "Poetry is the plough that turns up time," Mandelstam states in "Slovo i kul'tura" [The word and culture].[98] This metaphor brings to mind Pound's Canto 47:

> ... think of plowing.
> By this gate art thou measured
> Thy day is between a door and a door
> Two oxen are yoked for plowing
> Or six in the hill field
> White bulk under olives, a score for drawing down stone,
> Here the mules are gabled with slate on the hill road.
> Thus was it in time.[99]

To be "in time" is to make the present actual and to revive the past. Both Pound in Canto 47 and Mandelstam in "The Horseshoe Finder" allude to Hesiod. Furthermore, in "The Horseshoe Finder," the seafarer is ploughing the sea: the metaphors "soggy furrows," "The soggy black soil of Neaira each night plowed anew," "The air can be as dark as water, and all creatures swim in it like fish / Whose fins thrust the sphere"—all show the relativity of the separation between land, sea, and air. Pound's "whale-path" and the "tracks of ocean" ("Seafarer") are not only metaphors comparable to those mentioned above, but they also reveal the similar poetic vision of the two poets, although I doubt that they had even heard of each other.

The end of Pound's "Seafarer" powerfully emphasizes the idea of uselessness of gathering treasures on earth as if alluding to Matthew 6:19 ("Lay not

---

97 Iurii Levin, "Zametki o 'krymsko-ellinskikh stikhakh' O. Mandel'shtama," in *Mandel'shtam i antichnost'* (Moscow: Rossiiskii gosudarstvennyi gumanitarnyi universitet, 1995), 91.

98 Mandelstam, CPL, 113.

99 Ezra Pound, "Canto 47," in his *The Cantos* (London: Faber and Faber, 1975), 237.

up for yourselves treasures upon earth, where moth and rust doth corrupt, and where thieves break through and steal"), which recalls Derzhavin's "The River of Time," his last unfinished ode, the title of which was "Na tlennost'" [On frailty], and Mandelstam's "The Horseshoe Finder":

> Human lips
> which have nothing more to say
> Keep the form of the last uttered word,
> And a feeling of heaviness fills the hand…
> [...]
> Some
> stamp lions on coins,
> Others
> a head.
> Various copper, bronze and golden lozenges
> Are buried in earth with equal honor.
> The age has tried to gnaw on them leaving the clench of its teeth.
> Time cuts me like a coin,
> And there is not enough of myself left for myself…

The image of time which "has tried to gnaw" on ancient coins is reminiscent of Bergson's image of time where the past "is gnawing into the future."[100] The Bergsonian coil symbolizes the real synchronic flux of time, *durée*: "Real duration gnaws on things and leaves on them the mark of its tooth."[101] In Mandelstam's poem, however, time "cuts me": the lyrical hero, if not the poet himself, is nearly factually cut by time.

Hence, time for Mandelstam, who is alluding to Derzhavin's "The River of Time" and to the theme of oblivion, is also a fearful thing. Derzhavin's poem is about the flux of time, which carries away all human deeds and "drowns in the chasm of oblivion / nations, kingdoms and kings." In his pessimistic view of time as the destroyer of all things, Derzhavin admits that the creations of poetic art will be the last things to be destroyed, but they will not last either: "Even if something is left / through the sounds of lyre and trumpet" (metonymies of lyrical and heroic poetry for Derzhavin), "it would be swallowed by eternity's muzzle / and won't escape the common fate."[102] As Mandelstam

---

100 Henri Bergson, *Matter and Memory* (New York: Doubleday, 1959), 52–53.

101 Idem, *Creative Evolution* (New York: Random House, 1944), 7, 52.

102 Interlinear translation is mine.

wrote, "Here, in the rusty language of doddering age, with all its power and perspicacity, the latent thought of the future is expressed—its loftiest lesson abstracted, its keystone sounded. This lesson is relativism, relativity: 'But if something should happen to remain.'"[103] Thus, the only way to escape oblivion is wandering in order to gain knowledge and reveal it in poetry, as Mandelstam in "The Age" welds together (literally, "glues together") "the vertebrae of two centuries." The poet who manages to weld together centuries and preserve "the tale of the tribe" is undefeatable.

Similar to the poet is the seafarer, who brings back knowledge, space and time, "liberates himself of future as well as of the past," to quote Eliot. The themes of wandering and spiritual quest are central in *The Cantos* and in Mandelstam's "Crimean" cycle, including "Insomnia. Homer. Tautly Swelling Sails," as Cavanagh observed.[104] Pound's Odysseus, like Mandelstam's, is sailing "after knowledge," although "Knowledge the shade of a shade, / Yet must you sail after knowledge / Knowing less than dragged beasts" (Canto 47).

Similarly, in his famous poem of 1917, "Insomnia. Homer. Tautly Swelling Sails . . ." Mandelstam penned the lines:

> And leaving his ship, canvas worn-out on the seas,
> Odysseus came back filled with time and space.[105]

Time and space are metonymies of knowledge and experience for Mandelstam, emphasizing the idea of returning and bringing back the knowledge acquired by hard work (*natrudivshii* means the one that has worked hard, not just worn-out, as one of the translators put it). In the poem "Insomnia. Homer. Tautly swelling sails . . ."[106] a chain of nominal sentences "performing" (or acting out), in the Mandelstamian dictum, a stream of consciousness, is at the same time a chain of metonymies of space, history, and culture. Cavanagh correctly notes that "Mandelstam's brief lyric, like Pound's 'First Canto,' evokes both the presence of the past and its pastness, as the events described in Homer's writings converge with and diverge from the experience of the modernist poet-synthesizer who works to recuperate an ancient history for the modern age."[107]

---

103   Mandelstam, CPL, 138.

104   Cf. Cavanagh, *Osip Mandelstam and the Modernist Creation*, 23–25.

105   Osip Mandelstam, *Poems*, trans. James Green (London: Harper Collins, 1980).

106   Idem, *50 Poems*, trans. Bernard Meares (New York: Persea Books, 1977).

107   Cavanagh, *Osip Mandelstam and the Modernist Creation*, 25.

"Insomnia" separated, though not completely, from "Homer" can be read as an expression of the poet's "nostalgia [or craving] for world culture" (Mandelstam's famous definition of Acmeism). "Homer," placed between "insomnia" and "tautly swelling sails," combines this craving with time, space, and history. "The catalogue of ships" that sailed to Troy, "sei vyvodok, sei poezd zhuravlinyi" [this outstretched brood, a train of cranes] is a link that connects epochs. In the lines "i more, i Gomer—vsë dvizhetsia liubov'iu" [both Homer and the sea: all things are moved by love], metonymy (Homer stands for *The Iliad* and *The Odyssey*, the sea for wandering), not metaphor, is the device that links "disparate ideas" (Lomonosov[108]). Both Pound in Canto I and Mandelstam in the above poem sing a hymn to love that gives meaning to wandering. However, the sea in Mandelstam's poem is not just "a metaphor of love," as Nielson put it,[109] but first and foremost a metonymy of a quest for time, if not for eternity, and for history. In addition, as was observed by Cavanagh,

> The sea itself, *móre* in Russian, is anagrammatically concealed within Homer, *Gomér*, while Homer, conversely, lies partially in the Russian "sea," as Mandelstam reminds us by rocking the two words back and forth in the poem's closing lines: "I mó-re, i Go-mér"; "I vot Go-mér molchit / I mó-re chérnoe. . . ." Centuries, traditions, and linguistic boundaries wash away in the verbal play that gives any Russian speaker permanent access to a Homeric past through their own sea, their móre.[110]

The last two verses of the poem, "And the dark sea thunders, eloquent, / And rumbling heavily it breaks beneath my bed,"[111] finally wash away the boundary between a sleepless night in Koktebel, where Mandelstam composed this

---

108 Mikhail Lomonosov (1711-1765), *Ritorika* (St. Petersburg: Imperatorskaia akademiia nauk, [1748]), §27, 111, cited in Tynianov, *Poetika*, 236. Mikhail Lomonosov (1711-1765) was a Russian polymath, scientist, and writer, who made important contributions to literature, education, and science. Among his discoveries were the atmosphere of Venus and the law of conservation of mass in chemical reactions. He laid down the foundations of the Russian rhetoric and poetics as well and was a great poet himself.

109 Cf. N. A. Nielson, "Bessonnitsa," in *Mandel'shtam i antichnost'* (Moscow: Rossiiskii gosudarstvennyi gumanitarnyi universitet, 1995), 65–76.

110 Cavanagh, *Osip Mandelstam and the Modernist Creation*, 25.

111 I would have translated this as "the Black Sea" and "head."

poem, and the siege of Troy. This merging represents a shift in time-space, symbolizing the integrity of time, space and history and making the closeness of historic epochs vivid and palpable.

For Mandelstam, eternity and heaven *are natural* and are achieved through art and poetry (my emphasis), from his early poems ("My breath, my warmth has been already / Laid upon the panes of eternity," 1909) to his last, written in exile in Voronezh after his first term in Stalin's prison and in anticipation of further persecution. Art gives Mandelstam the strength to leave space (and time, that is, the here and now):

> So I leave space for a desolate garden
> Of values and break at my will
> A seeming permanence and coherence of causes,
> And there, alone and tranquil,
>
> Infinity, I read your textbook,
> Which can offer solutions and heal,
> A leafless, primeval, wild heal-book,
> A task-book of infinite roots.[112]

Fear and Awe: Mandelstam's "The Slate Ode"

Unlike Mandelstam's "The Horseshoe Finder," in which, as discussed, all the similes and metaphors are revealed, and the successive flow of poetical thought reenacted in free verse, "The Slate Ode" is one of the poet's most esoteric works. Mandelstam is known for his exceptional manner of hiding allusions and destroying bridges-associations. If the theme of "The Horseshoe Finder" is wandering, that of "The Slate Ode" is a metaphysical quest:

> Here terror writes, here a shift writes
> With a leaden milky stick,
> Here a draft grows ripe
> Of the flowing water's disciples.
> [...]
>
> There a plumb-line preaches,
> Time gnaws, water teaches,

---

112 "Oktavy," 11, in Mandel'shtam, *Polnoe sobranie sochinenii i pisem*, 1:188 (translation is mine).

And a transparent wood of air
Has had a surfeit of them all.
[…]

Who am I? I am not a straight stonemason,
Neither a shipbuilder, nor a roofer,
I am a double-dealer, with a double soul,
A friend of night, and a daymonger.
Blessed is he who called flint
A disciple of the flowing water,
Blessed is he who tied the strap
Of the mountains' feet on firm soil.

So, now I study the record
Of the slate summer scratches,
The language of flint and air,
With a layer of darkness, a layer of light;
And I yearn to put my fingers
In the flinty way from the old song
As in a sore—to weld and join
Flint with water, a horseshoe with a ring. [113]
(1923)

In his profound book *An Approach to Mandelstam*, Ronen constructs diachronic and synchronic analyses of "The Slate Ode" and "January 1, 1924."[114] While restoring the connections between these Mandelstam's poems written in 1923, Ronen even created a kind of a history of Russian verse from Lomonosov and Derzhavin to the twentieth century. He also bridged together Mandelstam's prose, essays, and poetry. His writing is striking but sometimes superfluous, as he discusses allusions and associations not directly related to the poem under consideration such as, for example, his mentioning the use of the paronyms *blazhen* and *blagosloven* [blessed] in Russian poetry: after Derzhavin and especially Pushkin, there was hardly a Russian poet who did not use these words.[115] Mandelstam's stanza that uses these words will be discussed below.

---

113 Translation is mine. It appeared in full in *Brooklyn Rail: In Translation* (March 2011), http://intranslation.brooklynrail.org/russian/the-slate-ode.

114 See Ronen, *An Approach to Mandelstam*, 37–223.

115 Ibid., 200–201.

A close reading of a poem, linking each line with its sources, is not new but is probably one of the most productive methods of restoring the entire picture. This method allowed Ronen to bridge the gaps: to restore the allusions and associations hidden between the lines and even between the words. Ronen correctly links "The Slate Ode" and its very title with Derzhavin's "The River of Time," written on a slate tablet with a leaden chalk or "milky stick," to quote Mandelstam.[116] The poetic motive of Derzhavin's poem is the flux of time, which carries away all human deeds and "drowns in the chasm of oblivion / nations, kingdoms, and kings":

> Relentless River, coursing ages,
> Usurps all works of mortal hands;
> It thinks all worlds, in darkness rages:
> Should any trace endure an hour
> Through Lyre's chord or Trumpet's call,
> Obscured it drowns, by Time devoured,
> Purged of its from—the Fate of all...[117]

The motif of the flux of time erasing all traces of human activity and leading to oblivion is half hidden in allusions and associations, as "The Slate Ode" begins on a very high note: "Zvezda s zvezdoi—moguchii styk, / Kremnistyi put' iz staroi pesni" [A star and a star is a mighty joint, / A flinty way from an old song...], immediately reminding us of a Lermontov poem ("the old song" is a kind of a defamiliarization). Here is not only the motif of "poetic oblivion," as observed by Ronen, but also the idea and yearning for the connection of two worlds. This motif continues into the next two lines:

> Кремня и воздуха язык,
> Кремень с водой, с подковой перстень...
> [The tongue of flint and air,
> Flint with water, a horseshoe signet ring.]

Ronen quotes Mandelstam's idea from his "Conversation about Dante" where the Russian poet refers to Novalis: "The Hermit in Heinrich von

---

116 Ibid., 59.

117 Gavrila Derzhavin, *Poetic Works. A Bilingual Album*, trans. Alexander Levitsky and Martha T. Kitchen (Providence, RI: Brown University, 2001), 188.

Ofterdingen calls the miner's craft 'astrology turned inside out.' However, for Mandelstam, mineralogy and 'astrology' are one."[118]

According to Mandelstam, "Mineral rock is an impressionistic diary of weather accumulated by millions of natural disasters; however, it is not only of the past, but also of the future: it has periodicity. It is Aladdin's lamp penetrating the geological twilight dusk of future ages."[119] Analyzing these lines and their allusion to Lermontov's "skvoz' tuman kremnistyi put' blestit" [a flinty way glistens through the fog], Mikushevich mentions that "flint can hardly glisten through fog; it glistens due to the anagrammatically concealed meaning of the words: 'kremen'' [flint]—'ne merk' [does not wane]."[120] Mikushevich also points out that the word *kremen'* [flint] rhymes with *vremia* [time], while the "flinty way" is an analogue of "the river of time." He comments that the Russian word for time, *vremia*, is etymologically derived from the Sanskrit word *vartaman*, which means "way," "furrow," "to revolve," and hence Mikushevich concludes, "'A stream babbles back to its source'—this is the river of time going back to its source."[121]

> Обратно в крепь родник журчит
> Цепочкой, пеночкой и речью.
> [A stream babbles back to its source,
> Like a foamy warbler, a chain, a speech.]

Mandelstam's desire to unify time and thus overcome oblivion is revealed in these lines. In addition to the allusions to Derzhavin (the first two are allusions to the titles of his poems) and Pushkin analyzed by Ronen,[122] there is also the matter of the second meaning of the word *penochka* (it is not only the name of a bird, a wood warbler, but also a derivative from "foam;" both *penochka* and *tsepochka* [chain] are diminutive forms, and the fountain/spring (the foamy warbler) is a metaphor for poetry. The fountain of human thought and being (a striking resemblance to Shelley's "Mont Blanc") moves backwards:

---

118 Ronen, *An Approach to Mandelstam*, 65–66.

119 Mandelstam, CPL, 439.

120 Vladimir Mikushevich, "Dvoinaia dusha poeta v 'Grifel'noi ode' Mandel'shtama," in *Sokhrani moiu rech'* 3, no. 1 (2000): 58.

121 Ibid.

122 Ronen, *An Approach to Mandelstam*, 105.

this is not a mechanical metamorphosis. In an earlier poem Mandelstam wrote:

> Aphrodite, remain foam,
> A word come back to music.
> (*Silentium, 1910*)

The lines "Here terror writes, here a shift writes / With a leaden milky stick" have a circular movement (characteristic of Mandelstam, who was more than skeptical of the so-called linear causal chain of things). These lines connect the first and second stanzas and introduce the theme of inspiration and creativity. Ronen was right to present both a synchronic and diachronic interpretation of these lines, where fear itself does not have a physical, but primarily metaphysical meaning: the mysterious fear of the secrets of being and the "geological" shifts of time, as well as the fear and uncertainty of creativity known to every true master. As Mandelstam himself put it, "The horror of the present tense is given here, a kind of *terror praesentis*. Here, the unalloyed present is taken as a sign introduced to ward off evil [negation or *churanie*, in Mandelstamian dictum]. The present tense, completely isolated from both the future and the past, is conjugated like pure fear, like danger."[123]

The "leaden milky stick," again, in a circular movement, connects Derzhavin's poem to the first stanza, with Mandelstam's perception of being as becoming, as a school of knowledge and creativity. Growing and learning is compared to ripening: "Here a draft grows ripe / Of the disciples of flowing water." The metaphorical use of the verb "to ripen" is crucial for Mandelstam, who connects creativity, understood as a process (he therefore wrote in "Conversation about Dante" that "the drafts cannot be annihilated"[124]), with natural phenomena, for example, with the ripening of the grapes.

Mandelstam spent much of his time in the Crimea before the revolution of 1917 and later in 1919–1920. The motifs of "steep goatish towns," of "sheepish villages and churches," and of "the mighty layering of flint" (the epithet "mighty," as Ronen noticed, is used twice in "The Slate Ode" and in "January 1, 1924") as well as the images in "The Horseshoe Finder" and other poems ("Theodosia," for instance) were inspired by Mandelstam's Crimean visits. As Mandelstam put it, "The Black Sea pebbles tossed up on shore by the rising

---

123 Mandelstam, CPL, 403.
124 Mandel'shtam, *Polnoe sobranie sochinenii i pisem*, 2:429.

tide helped me immensely when the conception of this conversation was taking shape. [. . .] It was thus that I came to understand that mineral rock is something like a diary of the weather, like a meteorological blood clot."[125]

While "the mighty layering of flint" is a development of the motif from the first stanza, "plumbline the preacher" (or plumb-ruler), connects two worlds, the physical and the metaphysical, and alludes to Mandelstam's own "The Horseshoe Finder" ("A plumbline of a mariner") and to his essay "Petr Chaadaev" (1928), as pointed out by Ronen.[126] The juxtaposition of "multi-colored day" and "hawkish night," which "carries a burning chalk / And feeds the slate to erase / The day's impressions away / From the iconoclastic board," is, again, the opposition of physical everyday life to metaphysical being. Night as beneficial to poetic and prophetic inspiration is a common motif in Russian lyrical poetry. The night is bringing "burning chalk": this metaphor connects the theme of Derzhavin's poem with the whole tradition of Russian lyrical poetry. Ronen quotes a dozen poems to which this image alludes. Mandelstam, perhaps, did not think consciously about all of them, but they were in his poetic "blood." There is one, however, yet to be mentioned: Lermontov's "A Word Born of Fire and Light." The aim of the poet according to Mandelstam—and here he speaks mainly of he poet and poetry—is "to erase / The day's impressions away / from the iconoclastic board / And shake off transparent visions / Like nestlings from the hand!" "Transparent," *prozrachnyi*, stands perhaps in opposition to the *prizrachnyi* ["seeming"] experiences and impressions of the day. Taranovsky, in his analysis of the poems "Kogda Psikheya-zhizn'" [When Psyche-life] and "Petropolis," emphasizes the opposition of "transparent spring" and "transparent death."[127] This interpretation of poetry as vision and foresight (connecting poetic and prophetic inspiration) is very close to the ideas expressed by Shelley in his "Defense of Poetry" who argued that "Poets [. . .] were called in the earlier epochs of the world legislators or prophets."[128] For Mandelstam, a poet is a disciple of a prophet if not a prophet himself.

---

125   Mandelstam, CPL, 438.

126   Ronen, *An Approach to Mandelstam*, 120–121.

127   Taranovsky, *Essays on Mandelstam*, 157.

128   Percy Bysshe Shelley, "A Defence of Poetry," in *Shelley's Poetry and Prose*, ed. Donald H. Reiman and Sharon B. Powers (New York: Norton, 1977), 482. In addition, Shelley states that the poet "not only beholds intensely the present as it is, and discovers those laws according to which present things ought to be ordered, but he beholds the future in the present, and his thoughts are the germ of the flower and the fruit of the latest time."

The entire second part of "The Slate Ode" is a development of this theme of prophetic inspiration. Important for the interpretation of the poem is, therefore, the stanza beginning with the lines "It is only by the voice that we'll know / What scribbled and struggled there / And lead a stiff lead pencil where / The voice will point out," which was omitted in "Khardzhiev's" version.[129] I agree with Ronen, who gives both versions of the poem (with and without this stanza) in his book.

The fifth stanza begins with the motif of day and alludes to some of Mandelstam's earlier poems (starting with "The Horseshoe Finder"), reaching far beyond the limits of a linear interpretation of time. One can read "The tender game" [*babki*, a national Russian game similar to baseball] of children in the context of "The Horseshoe Finder" (written not long before "The Slate Ode"), where "children are playing with the vertebrae of extinct animals." Here again, Mandelstam reveals the footprints of the past in the present and expresses a kind of cosmic vision, which he praised highly in Tiutchev.

As noted above, between the sixth and the seventh stanzas in the draft of the "Ode" there were these lines (restored in Metz's and in Lekmanov's editions[130]):

It is only by the voice that we'll know
What scribbled and struggled there
And lead a stiff lead pencil where
The voice will lead us and show.
I break the night, a burning chalk
To make a steadfast instant note,
I trade the noise for the arrows' song,
I trade harmony for a strembling wrath.

Moreover, having compared the drafts, Alexander Mets convincingly demonstrated how "The Slate Ode" developed from the seven–stanza structure to nine stanzas.[131] In the process of multiple revisions, Mandelstam also dropped overt allusions to the Sermon on the Mount (Matthew 5:7): "Mountainous bell-ringing garden [Nagornyi kolokol'nyi sad]" and "Calling

129 Nikolai Khardzhiev (1903–1996), a writer and a scholar, was the first editor of the official Soviet Mandelstam edition of 1973 after a long period of silence. See bibliography.

130 Mandel'shtam, *Polnoe sobranie sochinenii i pisem*, 1:135; and Mandel'shtam, *Sobranie stikhotvorenii 1906–1937*, 165. See also Mets, *Osip Mandel'shtam i ego vremia*, 153-230.

131 Mets, *Osip Mandel'shtam i ego vremia*, 153–230.

[or founding] the Flinty Mountainous Lyceum [Mandelstam used the Russian transliteration of the Greek word *lykeion*] / Of the disciples of the flowing water [Kremnevykh gor sozvat' likei / uchenikov vody protochnoi]."[132] As was correctly observed by Mikhail Gasparov, "The key images that connected 'The Slate Ode' with Derzhavin's octave, the foundational background of Mandelstam's poem, are wiped out from the latter step by step."[133] Moreover, the Romantic idea that poetic gift is akin to prophetic vision, as in Shelley's "Defense of Poetry," was perhaps unacceptable to the mature Mandelstam. Since all his poems of that period changed in intensification of the activity of the lyrical "I," as noted by Gasparov,[134] the "The Slate Ode" thus symbolizes a shift from the half-tones and hidden allusions of the books *Stone* and *Tristia* to a more active social position. It is not a "passive" contemplation: like Derzhavin, Mandelstam "breaks the night" with the "burning chalk" and therefore "trades the noise" (*The Noise of Time*, the title of his book in prose) for "the arrow's song," and "harmony" for "trembling wrath" (or "strembling," since Mandelstam coins a neologism, very much like Khlebnikov, changing "trembling" to its opposite. Originally, the word *strepet* [strembling] was a typist's error for *trepet* [trembling], which Mandelstam liked.[135]

To learn from memory means to learn "to listen and to hear the voices": this line returns to the theme of the poet and poetry. In fact, the whole poem evokes this theme through the motifs of time-space, the sense of history, the ability to listen, to hear the voices, and to learn. Hence the constant shifts from "we" to "I" in the second part of the ode, beginning with the sixth stanza in which the lyrical hero of the poem (who in this case is very close to the poet himself) is already present:

> Who am I? I am not a straight stonemason,
> Neither a shipbuilder, nor a roofer,

---

132 Ibid., 178.

133 Mikhail Gasparov, "'Solominka' Mandelshtama. Poetika chernovika," in his *Izbrannye stat'i* (Moscow: NLO, 1995), 188. Gasparov offers a similar idea in his essay "'Za to chto ia ruki tvoi . . .'—stikhotvorenie s otbroshennym kliuchom" ["Because I could not hold your hands . . ."—a poem with a discarded key], ibid., 220. Cf. Irina Semenko, *Poetika pozdnego Mandel'shtama* (Moscow: Mandel'shtamovskoe obshchestvo, 1997), 9–35.

134 Gasparov, Grazhdanskaia lirika Mandel'shtama, 14–15, 109.

135 See notes to the poem in Osip Mandel'shtam, *Sochineniia v dvukh tomakh*, ed. Pavel Nerler, notes by A. D. Mikhailov and P. Nerler (Moscow: Khudozhestvennaia literatura, 1990), 498.

I am a double-dealer, with a double soul,
A friend of night, and a daymonger.

Ronen connects these lines with Pushkin's poem "My Pedigree" and with the dialogue of the clowns from *Hamlet* (act 5, scene 1): "What is he that builds stronger than either the mason, the shipwright, or the carpenter?" (Ronen omits the witty-paradoxical answer: "The gallows-maker; for that frame outlives a thousand tenants.") In my opinion, the ties to Mandelstam's own work revealed by Ronen (the poem "Actor and Worker," 1920, and his essay "The Bloody Mystery-Play of January Ninth," 1922) as well as the development of the "Orphic" theme (connected with Viacheslav Ivanov's essay "Orpheus") are much more important than allusions to *Hamlet* or even Pushkin's poem "My Pedigree").[136] Yet, only at the end of his long explication does Ronen briefly mention such typically Russian (or rather "Soviet") as well as Mandelstamian phrases as "Ia nochi drug, ia dnia zastrelshchik" which can be translated as: "I am a friend of the night, I am a 'shooter' of the day" ("the day's assailant," and even killer, but also "initiator," "beginner" of the day). Both meanings would be immediately caught by a native speaker living in the country of "newspeak," bored by endless editorials and broadcasting programs. Mandelstam plays with both meanings by "defamiliarizing" the words' monosemantic simplicity and hiding in irony his negative attitude towards reality. I dared to coin a word "daymomger" to render both meanings.

The following lines begin the coda of the entire poem:

Блажен, кто называл кремень
Учеником воды проточной.
Блажен, кто завязал ремень
Подошве гор на твёрдой почве.

Blessed is he who called flint
A disciple of the flowing water,
Blessed is he who tied the strap
Of the mountains' feet on firm soil.

They return to the themes of memory, mineralogy, and astrology, and also connect to chapter six of the "Conversation about Dante": "O Poetry, envy crystallography, bite your nails in anger and impotence! For it is recognized

---

136 Ronen, An Approach to Mandelstam, 193–200.

that the mathematical formulas necessary for describing crystal formation are not derivable from three-dimensional space. You are denied even that element of respect which any piece of mineral crystal enjoys."[137]

When discussing Mandelstam's use of *blazhen* and *blagosloven* [blessed], as mentioned above, Ronen displays brilliant knowledge of Russian literature and cites Russian poetry and prose from the Beatitudes ("Beatus ille qui") to Derzhavin, Pushkin, Chaadayev, Tiutchev, and Khodasevich.[138] However, he missed perhaps the most important allusion, to Derzhavin's rendering of Psalm 1, entitled "True Happiness":

> Most blessed is he who sitteth not
> In council with the men of slaughter,
> Nor standeth in the sinners' plot,
> Nor goeth down to their dark quarters.
> [...]
>
> As by the current of clear stream
> A tree is planted in the valley,
> Set 'round with colored blooms agleam,
> In season yielding fruitful tally [139]

Since we encounter here another "clear stream," it would be appropriate to link Mandelstam's poem to the Old Testament and to Derzhavin's "True Happiness." The lines "A stream babbles back to its source, / Like a foamy warbler, a chain, a speech" then become transparent: the poet, as a disciple, returns to Derzhavin, his source, while speech returns to "the Word which was in the beginning" (John 1:1).

Of the many allusions cited by Ronen, the most important is to Tiutchev: "Blazhen, kto posetil sei mir / V ego minuty rokovye [Blessed is he who came to this world in its most fateful moments]."[140] While explicating the last two lines of the above stanza, Ronen rightfully links them to the New Testament, referring to Mark 1:7, Luke 3:16, John 1:27, as well as Matthew 3:11, which "agrees well both with the theme of discipleship (because the office of touching, carrying, or untying the sandals was performed by the disciples for their

---

137 Mandelstam, CPL, 422.

138 Ronen, *An Approach to Mandelstam*, 200–213.

139 Derzhavin, *Poetic Works*, 25. Translated by Alexander Levitsky and Martha T. Kitchen.

140 Ronen, *An Approach to Mandelstam*, 201.

instructors)."[141] However, we should not overlook an allusion to Proverbs 30:4: "Who hath ascended up into heaven, or descended? who hath gathered the wind in his fists? who hath bound the waters in a garment? who hath established all the ends of the earth? what is his name, and what is his son's name, if thou canst tell?" The Russian edition of the Old Testament uses the same word *zaviazal* [tied, bound] that Mandelstam employs in "The Slate Ode": "Kto zaviazal vodu v odezhdu?" This allusion perhaps makes the poet the disciple of the Creator Himself.

In the last stanza, the poet speaks of himself as a disciple of memory, studying "a record / Of the summer scratches on the slate board, / The language of flint and air, / With a layer of darkness, a layer of light" (an allusion to mineralogy) in order "to put his fingers / In the flinty way from the old song, / As in a sore—to weld and join / Flint with water, a horseshoe with a ring." The circle is complete: the last stanza is like a spherical mirror reflecting the first one or, perhaps, it is another turn of the gyre. The word "sore, ulcer," as mentioned by Ronen, reveals the motif of painful inspiration, which, again, is one of the recurrent motifs in Russian poetry and alludes to the prophecies of Isaiah.[142] The poetic motive of "The Slate Ode" connects with the motive of "The River of Time," Lermontov's "Flinty Way," and "A Word Born of Fire and Light..." with its theme of the poet's duty and destiny to bridge gaps and overcome the metaphysical fear of loneliness and separation of mankind in history. It is not physical fear nor synchronic local time (even if it is a century)—these themes dominate "January 1, 1924," which, though powerful, is more "earthly" than the cosmic vision of "The Slate Ode." "The Slate Ode" reveals time-space, history, and being in their integrity. Here, Mandelstam goes far beyond "the Gates of Hercules": these are not only the gates of space, but also of time and being.

---

141   Ibid., 208.
142   Ibid., 221.

On Translating Mandelstam

According to Mandelstam, poetical speech can be heard in a very relative way because in a true work of poetry we hear many voices. One of them, a musical voice, is deaf without a word; another, narrative, is absolutely meaningless without music and images and can be retold as a dull story (that is the best proof of the absence of poetry); the other voice, metaphorical, expresses nothing without poetical motive and meaning revealed in a definite context.

Words acquire meaning only in the specific definite contexts, not in the dictionary. Like Benjamin, I think that words have "emotional connotations." Benjamin showed that the "word 'Brot' means something different to a German than the word 'pain' to a Frenchman, that these words are not interchangeable for them, that, in fact, they strive to exclude each other."[1]

I have a completely different approach to translation as compared to several other translations of Osip Mandelstam, to poetry, and to literary translation, even to prose, in general. It is my contention that the word as such is untranslatable even in prose. As George Steiner mentioned, there is no such vehicle that can transport a word literally into another language. Even composing in one's own language is an impossible task. Imitations, adaptations or free translations, which are of no time as poetry itself, on the other hand, do not attempt to render the original poem as translation as such into another language. What one can try is to render what Steiner calls in *After Babel* "a contingent motion of spirit."[2]

Consequently, literary translation is not literal. However, we must try to preserve what I would call an "image-picture" and, of course, the rhythm and energy of the poem, what I would also call "synergy." Thus, for instance, while

---

1   Walter Benjamin, "The Task of the Translator," in *Illuminations*, ed. Hanna Arendt, trans. Harry Zohn (New York: Schocken Books, 1969), 74.

2   George Steiner, *After Babel. Aspects of Language and Translation* (New York: Oxford UP, 1975), 71.

translating Osip Mandelstam's "Age," I would consider it more appropriate to translate *zver'* as "beast," not as "animal."[3] In the stanza

> Чтобы вырвать век из плена,
> Чтобы новый мир начать,
> Узловатых дней колена
> Нужно флейтою связать.
>
> Это век волну колышет
> Человеческой тоской,
> И в траве гадюка дышит
> Мерой века золотой.

    I believe it is inappropriate to translate literally "from captivity" ("To tear the age of captivity."[4] In both translations, in my opinion, the rhythm and energy are lost because of the acatalectic accent in "captivity" or literal translation of "in order," and in the lines "It is the age that caresses the wave / With human melancholy . . ." both rhythm and meaning are transformed since it is not "melancholy," but "angst," "anguish." Peter France rendered these lines as "It is the age rocking the wave / with the grief of humankind," which is more adequate. This is my attempt at translating this stanza:

> To tear the age from bounds,
> To start a new world,
> The knotty joints of days
> Should be bound by flute sounds.
> The age sways waves
> With a human angst that stings,
> While the adder breathes in the grass
> With a golden measure of things.

    Although literal translation is impossible, one has to do research and consider the work of the poet and particular poems in the historical context. Hence, it should be known that in his youth, Osip Mandelstam held left radi-

---

3   Osip Mandelstam, *Modernist Archaist: Selected Poems*, essay by Kevin M. F. Platt, trans. Charles Bernstein, Bernard Meares, Clarence Brown, Eugene Ostashevsky, Kevin M. F. Platt, and W. S. Merwin (Culver City, CA: Whale & Star, 2008).

4   Idem, *Poems of Osip Mandelstam*, trans. Peter France (New York: New Directions, 2014), 35. Ostashevsky uses the same word in Mandelstam, *Modernist Archaist*, 71.

cal views, joined the Socialist Revolutionary Party (SR) in 1907[5] and greeted both the February and, at first, even the October Revolution. Therefore, it would be inadequate to translate the lines "Voskhodish' ty v glukhiie gody— / O solnntse, sudiia, narod" as "In the dull years of stagnation / you rise up, people, judge, and sun."[6] Mandelstam saw those years (the poem was written in May 1918) as turbulent, troublesome, full of violence, but by no means were they "dull years of stagnation" for him. It was rather a "deadly time."

Robert Frost once said, "Poetry is what gets lost in translation." Charles Bernstein, the Bollingen Prize winner for 2019, claims that "poetry is found in translation." Hence, there are several types of translation: imitation, adaptation, and translation per se.

In his essay "Ikonostas" [Iconostasis], Rev. Pavel Florensky (1882– 1937), an outstanding Russian theologian, philosopher, and poet, who also perished in the GULAG, describes two types of creativity: the first, according to Florensky, is inspired by God and is a transition from the world of being into a higher world; the second, mechanistic type, is limited by earthly life and and human existence. He compares these two types of creativity to human dreams: in dreams of the second type, the soul ascends from earth to Heaven, it still has stronger ties with human existence than with God; but in dreams of the first type, the soul descends from Heaven to earthly life and brings "divine visions to earth."[7]

Florensky compares the art of icon painting to the art of translation from the divine language into an earthly human tongue. Icon painters, according to Florensky, have divine vision while copyists have only technique.[8] Every kind of creativity may be described as either a divine inspiration or a technical process. In this respect we may say that art is an impossible, an inaccessible thing. The work of art is revealed—or rather released—only after an endless struggle between the ideal as seen by an artist and its incarnation in a definite context either on canvas or on paper, no matter how it is written: with the help of oil, letters, or musical notes. As was stated by the Russian scholar Mikhail Bakhtin, "Creative art in its relation towards material is overcoming it [. . .] by means of

---

5   *Letopis'*, 26.

6   Mandelstam, *Poems of Osip Mandelstam*, 26.

7   Pavel Florensky, "Ikonostas," in his *Sobraniie sochinenii* [Collected works] (Paris: YMCA-Press, 1985), 1:203–204.

8   Ibid., 241–242.

the immanent improvement," that is to say, "With the help of creative artistic devices existing in the material of the art."[9] Thus a poet overcomes the word with the help of the language (that is, not with the help of "negative overcoming as it is done in the spheres of cognition: by the usage of algebraization, abbreviations, and conventional signs").[10]

Kafka was haunted by the same idea of the impossibility of art, the impossibility of writing, which was directly connected to the heritage and curse of Babel. He expressed it to Max Brod in 1921 when he was speaking about "the impossibility of not writing, the impossibility of writing in German, the impossibility of writing differently. One could almost add a fourth impossibility: the impossibility of writing."[11]

Literary translation and especially the translation of poetry is, philosophically speaking, the same impossible and inaccessible task. Yet, the creative individual has always been tempted by the idea of the impossible, by the ideal. As was expressed by Mandelstam, "there is nothing like this in Russian, but it should be in Russian."[12] That is why literary or creative translation exists alongside word-for-word or grammatical translation. The translation of poetry is still much more complicated and subtle than the translation of prose: a translator of poetry is trying, if we might say, quoting the line from Cesar Vallejo's poem, "to seize the poet [by his hand] in the act of creating poetry."[13]

One of the tasks of the translator (or rather super-tasks) is to restore the bridges, the ties between the humanity destroyed after the fall of the Tower of Babel. As Dante expressed it in *De Vulgari Eloquentia*,

> Since it is our wish to enlighten to some extent the discernment of those who walk through the streets like blind men, generally fancying

---

9   Mikhail Bakhtin, "Problema soderzhaniia, materiala i formy v slovesnom khudozhestvennom tvorchestve," in *Voprosy literatury i estetiki* (Moscow: Khudozhestvennaia literatura, 1975), 46.

10 Ibid., 59 (translation is mine).

11 Kafka, cited in Steiner, *After Babel*, 65.

12 Osip Mandelstam, "Slovo i kul'tura" [Word and culture] and "Razgovor o Dante" [Conversation about Dante], in his *Slovo i kul'tura* (Moscow: Sovetskii pisatel', 1987), 41 (translation is mine.)

13 César Vallejo, *The Complete Poetry. A Bilingual Edition*, ed. and trans. Clayton Eshleman (Berkeley, CA: University of California Press, 2007), 423.

that those things which are [really] in front of them are behind them, we will endeavor, the Word aiding us from heaven, to be of service to the vernacular speech; not only drawing the water of our own wit for such a drink, but mixing with it the best of what we have taken or compiled from others, so that we may thence be able to give draughts of the sweetest hydromel.[14]

This is close to the phenomenological approach towards translation as Walter Benjamin understood it. Probably, "in the end of history," all separate languages will fuse again or will come back to the "Word which was in the beginning.[15]"

I am taking into consideration the Russian formalist scholar Yuri Tynianov's attempt to differentiate poetry from prose by emphasizing that "it is exactly the unity and density of the sequence which is an objective characteristic of poetic rhythm."[16] This definition actually coincides with that of Ezra Pound's: "Poetry [. . .] is the most concentrated form of verbal expression."[17] Furthermore, there is a striking affinity in both Mandelstam's and Pound's views on the nature of poetry. In "Conversation about Dante," Mandelstam asserts,

It is only with the severest qualifications that poetic discourse or thought may be referred to as "sounding"; for we hear in it only the crossing of two lines, one of which, taken by itself, is completely mute, while the other, abstracted from its prosodic transmutation, is totally devoid of significance and interest, and is susceptible of paraphrasing, which, to my mind, is surely a sign of non-poetry. For where there is amenability to paraphrase, there the sheets have never been rumpled, there poetry, so to speak, has never spent the night.[18]

Pound, in turn, distinguishes "three kinds of poetry":

---

14   Dante, "De Vulgari Eloquentia," in *Classical and Medieval Literary Criticism*, ed. A. Preminger, O. B. Hardison, Jr., and K. Kerraine (New York: Unger, 1974), 412 (emphasis added).

15   John 1:1.

16   Iurii Tynianov, *Problema stikhotvornogo iazyka* (Moscow: Sovetskii pisatel', 1965), 66.

17   Pound, *ABC*, 36.

18   Mandelstam, CPL, 397.

MELOPŒIA, wherein the words are charged, over and above their plain meaning, with some musical property, which directs the bearing of trend of that meaning.

PHANOPŒIA, which is a casting of images upon their visual imagination.

LOGOPŒIA, "the dance of the intellect among words.[19]

In the *ABC of Reading*, Pound maintains, very much like Mandelstam, that "music rots when it gets too far from the dance. Poetry atrophies when it gets too far from music."[20] Hence, for Pound and Mandelstam the nature of poetry is inseparable from music, the understanding of which goes far beyond meter and rhythm for both poets. According to Mandelstam, poetical speech can be heard in a very relative way because in a true work of poetry we hear many voices, one of which, a musical voice, is deaf without a word; another, narrative, is absolutely meaningless without music and images and can be re-told as a dull story (that is the best proof of the absence of poetry); the other voice, metaphorical, expresses nothing without poetical motive and meaning revealed in a definite context. This thought of the Russian poet coincides to some extent with Gerard Manley Hopkins's definition of verse as of "speech wholly or partially repeating the same figure of sound."[21] To name the phenomena of the world is to reveal them. Revelation is re-evaluation: re-veiling and unveiling something so palpable and fragile that when "rendered in a disdainful prose," to quote Pushkin, it evaporates.

Translating the poems of Osip Mandelstam is even more impossible since his poetry is not only full of allusions and hidden and direct citations (as, for instance, allusions to Pindar in "The Horseshoe Finder"), but it is also esoteric, and the bridges–associations between metaphors are in most cases eliminated, as in "The Slate Ode" or in "The Octaves." Hence, the translator of Mandelstam's poetry has to do a lot of research but then thoroughly "hide" the acquired knowledge between the lines, since translation differs from interpretation, although the latter is also implied.

---

19 Ezra Pound, *Literary Essays*, ed. T. S. Eliot (London: Faber & Faber, 1954, rpt. 1985), 25 (hereafter LE).

20 Pound, *ABC*, 61.

21 Bernadette Waterman Ward, *World as Word. Philosophical Theology in Gerard Manley Hopkins* (Washington, D.C.: The Catholic Univerity of America Press, 2002), 175.

It is said that a translator is like a spy: if everything is fine, the author of the original is praised and the translator is barely noticed; if not, the translator is blamed. Having that in mind, I am going to discuss several translations of Osip Mandelstam's "Stalin's Epigram," which cost him two exiles and, eventually, life.

The original text is arranged in two stanzas, eight lines each, as if looking forward to his famous "Octaves" the first draft of which he composed in 1933 as well. Unlike the later deep metaphysical and esoteric poem, the epigram is written in an overt manner with a lot of colloquial expressions, idioms, and even neologisms coined by the poet. It comprises alternating rhymed couplets (hence the translators changed the graphic appearance of the poem). The basic meter is alternating anapest, the first two lines are four-feet with catalectic or masculine rhymes, the third and fourth are three-feet with acatalectic or feminine rhymes, the fifth and fourth are four-feet catalectic (masculine) again and so forth. Meter and rhyme are crucial for Mandelstam in general, especially in the poem under consideration, since it is based on colloquial idioms and its rhythm and rhymes remind that of "folk" couplets; hence the poet uses first person plural point of view, that of collective "we." In the selections quoted below, three translations are unrhymed: that by Clarence Brown and W. S. Merwin, by David McDufff, and by John Simkin; there are occasional rhymes in Scott Horton's adaptation, while Dmitry Smirnov and I tried to preserve rhymes.

The idiomatic tone is set in the very first two lines in which Mandelstam coins idioms of his own. The phrase "not to feel the country" deconstructs two well-known idioms: "nog pod soboi ne chuiat'": to be running very fast or to be flying, often to be beside oneself with joy (literally, "not to feel one's feet"), but also: to be run off one's feet, to be extremely exhausted. However, Mandelstam creates a new meaning that implies "running without looking back from fear" and "being deaf and dumb," since the Russian *chuiat'* also means "to hear" and "to feel." This meaning is extended and developed in the second line: "our speeches cannot be heard at ten paces." Both meanings are rendered by the translators correctly, with the little exception that in Clarence Brown's and W. S. Merwin's translation the active voice is changed into the passive: where Mandelstam has "we do not feel (hear)," Brown and Merwin say "our lives don't feel." In McDuff's translation words such as "inaudible" or "conversation" destroy, in my view, rhythm and music from the start, making it a literal translation.

The key image of the second "couplet" is that of Stalin's, of course: he was born and raised in Georgia, in the Caucasus; hence, he is "highlander," not "a mountaineer," which may imply some kind of athletic competition. It is notable that at that time there were several other Georgian-born Communist party functionaries alive, for instance, Sergo Ordzhonikidze who would be killed in 1937, member of the so-called Political Bureau of the Central Committee and the minister of heavy industry; however, the reader would unmistakably identify the unnamed "highlander" with Stalin. Scott Horton used the slang word "hillbilly," which is fresh but may sound a bit regional. I tried to use the word "highlander," while Dmitry Smirnov elegantly evaded the challenge by rhyming "occasion" and "Caucasian":

> But if people would talk on occasion,
> They should mention the Kremlin Caucasian.

It should be noted, however, that Osip Mandelstam used the word "osetina" [Osette], not "Caucasian," which unlike American English (as in the census), denotes ethnicity, not race, and may have some derogative and xenophobic, if not racist, implications since the people from the Caucasus are even now viewed and treated differently than ethnic Russians and the people of Slavic origin.

Further, it is said that the poet-functionary Demyan Bedny (real name Efim Aleksandrovich Pridvorov, 1883–1945), who was friendly with Stalin and gave him books to read, once mentioned that Stalin returned books soiled with oily fingers, after which the poet fell out of favor, but was not persecuted further. Most of the translators did not encounter any serious problems with rendering that image. Brown and Merwin have "The ten thick worms his fingers / His words like measures of weight." David McDufff's version is

> His thick fingers are fatty like worms,
> but his words are as true as pound weights.

Horton found the word "slimy":

> They're like slimy worms, his fat fingers,
> His words, as solid as weights of measure.

Dmitry Smirnov rhymed:

> His thick fingers are bulky and fat like live-baits,
> And his accurate words are as heavy as weights.

My version is:

> Like worms his thick fingers are fat,
> His words like pound weights are correct.

The famous children's poet Kornei Chukovsky wrote a long poem *Tarakanishche* [Giant cockroach] about the cockroach dictator with a giant moustache who was easily crushed in the end by a "brave sparrow," not by bigger animals. Everybody understood the implication, but it was Mandelstam who combined all the features adding Stalin's habit of wearing a military uniform without shoulder straps (only during great holidays Stalin would put on a field marshal's, and later, a generalissimo's uniform). One of Stalin's long-term associates, Vasily Molotov (real name Skryabin), prime-minister in 1930–1941, and minister of foreign affairs in 1939–1949 and 1953–1956, who signed the infamous Molotov-Ribbentrop Pact, had a very thin neck; hence "chicken-necked," as Brown and Merwin rendered, is correct, while "thick-skinned," which appears in McDuff's translation, is evidently not. Mandelstam further creates a Russian fairy-tale-like phantasmagoria turning half-men into demons, poltergeists, and evil spirits. Again, Clarence Brown's and W. S. Merwin's translation is more exact both rhythmically and semantically than that of McDuff's, which is like an exact interlinear translation, especially in his last but one couplet in which he destroys the music completely.

Again, the images of Scott Horton are more exact:

> In his cockroach moustaches there's a hint
> Of laughter, while below his top boots gleam.
>
> Round him a mob of thin-necked henchmen,
> He pursues the enslavement of the half-men.

Dmitry Smirnov kept the rhyme and meter:

> But around him a crowd of thin-necked henchmen,
> And he plays with the services of these half-men.

The real problem is Mandelstam's neologism *babachit*, which was probably coined on the basis of that grim old man Babai from nursery rhymes with which the parents tried to put kids to sleep or make them behave well: "If you don't behave, old Babai will go after you." Most of the translators just evaded the challenge: "He pokes out his finger and he alone goes boom" (Brown and Merwin), "but he just bangs and pokes" (McDufff), "One whimpers, another warbles, / A third miaows, but he alone prods and probes" (Horton), while Dmitry Smirnov tried to rhyme:

> Some are whistling, some meowing, some sniffing,
> He's alone booming, poking and whiffing.

As for me, I tried to use the word "boking" (from Oxford English Dictionary), which also has a meaning of "frighten" in addition to poking.

The word *ukaz* means "decree" in English and goes back to the time of Ivan the Terrible, if not earlier. Etymologically, it is derived from the verb *ukazyvat'*, which means "to show" or "to order." It is notable that the manuscript as well as the authorized editions of *Collected Works* of Mandelstam read "grants a decree after a decree," not "forges" (like a horseshoe in a forge). Perhaps it is linked to the Russian belief that a horseshoe brings happiness (in that meaning the word is used in Osip Mandelstam's Pindaric fragment "The Horseshoe Finder").

The biggest problem, however, is the last couplet in which Mandelstam coined another new idiom. The word "raspberry" in thief jargon means "a criminal underworld," usually that of thieves; it is a well-known fact now that Koba (Stalin's past criminal and then Bolshevik party name) was robbing postal carriages, trains, and even banks. The "old Bolsheviks" were uneasy about that, but since they needed money, Lenin convinced them that Stalin "expropriated" the rich and gave money to the party (a Bolshevik Robin Hood of a kind). What seems even more important, however, is that the Russian idiom *ne zhizn' a malina* [life like a raspberry] means *la dolce vita*, "a sweet life." Mandelstam replaces "life" with "execution," thus rhyming them since the Russian for "execution" [*kazn'*] and life [*zhizn'*] form a slant dissonance rhyme. In my view, it is impossible to render images, especially idioms, literally into a foreign language; thus it is necessary to replace "raspberry," which does not have the above implication in English. Again, in Brown and Merwin's translation it is just:

He rolls the executions of his tongue like berries.
He wishes he could hug them like big friend back home.

Mcduff's translation is just awkward besides being inexact:

Whatever the punishment he gives—raspberries,
And the broad chest of an Osette.

Scott Horton's translation is not much better:

Wherever an execution's happening though—
there's raspberry, and the Ossetian's giant torso.

I would say again that literal is not literary. Thus, Dmitry Smirnov evaded the challenge again by paraphrasing:

Every killing for him is delight,
And Ossetian torso is wide.

At first, I was considering just "a piece of cake" or even "a raspberry cake," but then decided to move further and have chosen the English idiom "cakes and ale" and added a rhyme "jail," which is justifiable, in my view, since Stalin has long been associated with the development of the prison and concentration camp system. In the end, Mandelstam consciously chose "Ossete," even though Stalin was ethnically Georgian, because the Russian word *osetina* in comparison with *gruzina* has an extra syllable necessary for preserving the meter, not just the rhyme. It can be also justified since Stalin's paternal grandfather Vissarion Dzhugashvili is said to be Ossetian:

Like horseshoes, he grants his every decree
Poking some in the groin, in the brow, in the eye.
His executions are like cakes and ale,
His broad chest of Ossete eclipses the jail.

Although in my own translation I was not quite able to preserve anapest everywhere, I tried to preserve the rhyme and an alternation of longer and shot lines.

Ian Probstein,
New York, 2021

Осип Мандельштам
(1891–1938)
Избранные стихотворения

Osip Mandelstam
(1891–1938)
Selected Poems

Из книги «Камень»
(стихотворения 1908–1915)

* * *

Дано мне тело — что мне делать с ним,
Таким единым и таким моим?

За радость тихую дышать и жить
Кого, скажите, мне благодарить?

Я и садовник, я же и цветок,
В темнице мира я не одинок.

На стёкла вечности уже легло
Моё дыхание, моё тепло,

Запечатлеется на нём узор,
Неузнаваемый с недавних пор.

Пускай мгновения стекает муть —
Узора милого не зачеркнуть!

1909

From *Stone*
(poems of 1908–1915)

---

* * *

I am given a body—what should I
Do with it, so whole and so mine?

Tell me, whom should I praise
For a quiet joy to live and to breathe?

I am a gardener and a flower as well,
I am not alone in the world's prison-cell.

My breath, my warmth has been already
Laid upon the panes of eternity.

A pattern is imprinted thereon,
A pattern, recently unknown.

Let moment's dregs then trickle down like haze—
This dear pattern nothing can erase!

1909

* * *

Я ненавижу свет
Однообразных звезд.
Здравствуй, мой давний бред —
Башни стрельчатой рост!

Кружевом, камень, будь
И паутиной стань:
Неба пустую грудь
Тонкой иглою рань!

Будет и мой черёд —
Чую размах крыла.
Так — но куда уйдёт
Мысли живой стрела?

Или, свой путь и срок
Я, исчерпав, вернусь:
Там — я любить не мог,
Здесь — я любить боюсь . . .

1912

* * *

I hate the light
Of tedious stars.
Hail, my dream, my wild—
A lancet turret, rise!

Become stone, a lace,
A cobweb's light crest,
Pelt with a sharp lance
The sky's hollow breast!

My turn will come as well—
I feel a mighty wingspread.
Well, but whereto will
Fly my thought's arrowhead?

Or I'll return when
I spend my time and ways:
I could not love—then,
Here I dread love's malaise . . .

1912

* * *

Паденье — неизменный спутник страха,
И самый страх есть чувство пустоты.
Кто камни нам бросает с высоты —
И камень отрицает иго праха?

И деревянной поступью монаха
Мощёный двор когда-то мерил ты,
Булыжники и грубые мечты —
В них жажда смерти и тоска размаха…

Так проклят будь готический приют,
Где потолком входящий обморочен
И в очаге весёлых дров не жгут!

Немногие для вечности живут,
Но если ты мгновенным озабочен,
Твой жребий страшен и твой дом непрочен!

1912

* * *

The fall is a constant companion of fear
And fear itself is a sense of void.
Who throws stones from the heights at us here,
And the stone denies the burden of dust?

And with the wooden posture of a monk
You also measured a paved yard once:
Crude dreams and rude paving stones
Reveal our craving for flight and death!

So be damned Gothic shelter where
A visitor is bewitched by the ceiling
And merry firewood isn't burned in a grate.

Few live for eternity, but if you care
Only about a moment, fleeing,
Your house is shaky, dreadful is your fate!

1912

Айя-София

Айя-София — здесь остановиться
Судил Господь народам и царям!
Ведь купол твой, по слову очевидца,
Как на цепи, подвешен к небесам.

И всем векам — пример Юстиниана,
Когда похитить для чужих богов
Позволила эфесская Диана
Сто семь зелёных мраморных столбов.

Но что же думал твой строитель щедрый,
Когда, душой и помыслом высок,
Расположил апсиды и экседры,
Им указав на запад и восток?

Прекрасен храм, купающийся в мире,
И сорок окон — света торжество,
На парусах, под куполом, четыре
Архангела прекраснее всего.

И мудрое сферическое зданье
Народы и века переживёт,
И серафимов гулкое рыданье
Не покоробит тёмных позолот.

1912

Hagia Sophia

Hagia Sophia—it was commanded by the Lord
That here kings and nations halt amazed!
Your cupola, in the eyewitness' word,
As if towards heaven on a chain was raised.

Justinian has set a model for all ages
When Diana of Ephesus as a marvel
Allowed him to abduct for alien gods
One hundred seven verdant pillars made of marble.

But what was thinking your generous builder
When elevated both in mind and spirit
He set out your apses and exedrae to bewilder,
Pointing them towards West and East?

Beautiful is the temple bathing in the world,
And its forty windows are the triumph of light,
But the most beautiful of all are the four gold
Archangels on the pendentives on high.

And the wise spherical building
Will outlast the ages and nations will outlive,
And even seraphim's resonant weeping
Will not distort the dark gold leaf.

1912

* * *

…На луне не растёт
ни одной былинки,
На луне весь народ
Делает корзинки —
Из соломы плетёт
Лёгкие корзинки.

На луне полутьма
И дома опрятней.
На луне не дома —
Просто голубятни,
Голубые дома —
Чудо-голубятни…

1914

* * *

... Not a single blade
Grows on the moon,
All people plait
Baskets on the moon—
Plait light baskets
From soft stray.

It is twilight on the moon,
Its houses are neat;
They are not houses, but
Just pigeon-lofts;
Blue houses—
Wonder dovecots ...

1914

Посох

Посох мой, моя свобода —
Сердцевина бытия,
Скоро ль истиной народа
Станет истина моя?

Я земле не поклонился
Прежде, чем себя нашёл;
Посох взял, развеселился
И в далекий Рим пошёл.

Пусть снега на чёрных пашнях
Не растают никогда,
И печаль моих домашних
Мне по-прежнему чужда.

Снег растает на утёсах —
Солнцем истины палим…
Прав народ, вручивший посох
Мне, увидевшему Рим!

1914

The Wand

My wand, my sole freedom,
The core of my being, my life.
How soon will my truth become
The truth of my nation at home?

I did not bow to my land
Until I found my self;
I rejoiced and took my wand
And went to a faraway Rome.

Yet the snow will never melt
On the black plowland,
And the sorrow that my kin felt
I still cannot understand.

The snow will melt on the heights
Burned by the truth's sun, and
My people then were right
To grant me, who saw Rome, a wand.

1914

* * *

Уничтожает пламень
Сухую жизнь мою,
И ныне я не камень,
А дерево пою.

Оно легко и грубо;
Из одного куска
И сердцевина дуба,
И вёсла рыбака.

Вбивайте крепче сваи,
Стучите, молотки,
О деревянном рае,
Где вещи так легки!

1915

* * *

The fire destroys
My dry life,—
So now I sing
Wood, not stone.

It's light and rough:
The heart of oak
And a fisherman's oar
Are from one trunk.

Drive the piles tight,
The hammers, strike
Of a wooden Eden
Where things are so light!

1915

Из книги «Tristia»
(стихотворения 1916–1922)

Декабрист

— Тому свидетельство языческий сенат —
Сии дела не умирают!
Он раскурил чубук и запахнул халат,
А рядом в шахматы играют.

Честолюбивый сон он променял на сруб
В глухом урочище Сибири,
И вычурный чубук у ядовитых губ,
Сказавших правду в скорбном мире.

Шумели в первый раз германские дубы,
Европа плакала в тенётах,
Квадриги чёрные вставали на дыбы
На триумфальных поворотах.

Бывало, голубой в стаканах пунш горит,
С широким шумом самовара
Подруга рейнская тихонько говорит,
Вольнолюбивая гитара.

— Ещё волнуются живые голоса
О сладкой вольности гражданства!
Но жертвы не хотят слепые небеса:
Вернее труд и постоянство.

Всё перепуталось, и некому сказать,
Что, постепенно холодея,
Всё перепуталось, и сладко повторять:
Россия, Лета, Лорелея.

1917

From *Tristia*[*]
(poems of 1916–1922)

A Decembrist

—A pagan senate is a proof of it:
Such things will never die!—
He wrapped himself in a robe and puffed a pipe
While people played chess nearby.

He traded his ambitious dream for a wooden hut
In a God-forsaken Siberian nook,
Venomous lips that uttered the truth about
A woeful world clasped a fanciful chibouk.

The German oaks roared for the first time then,
And Europe wept in the snares,
The horses of black chariots pranced when
The triumphal quadrigae turned to wide squares.

Blue punch used to burn in broad glasses,
With a wide slush of the samovar
A friend spoke from the Rein's shores,
A freedom-loving guitar.

—Each living voice still anxiously cries:
Sweet civil rights and liberty!
But the blind skies don't want such sacrifice:
Persistence and labor are safer to rely.

All is mixed up, and there's no one to be told,
All is mixed up, and it is sweet to say,
While growing gradually cold:
Oh Russia, Lethe, Lorelei.

1917

---

[*] The *Tristia* is a collection of letters written in elegiac couplets by the Augustan poet Ovid during his exile from Rome to Pontus, in 8 AD. Osip Mandelstam supposed that Ovid was exiled to Taurida (Tavria), as the ancient Greeks called Crimea.

* * *

Когда в тёплой ночи замирает
Лихорадочный форум Москвы
И театров широкие зевы
Возвращают толпу площадям —

Протекает по улицам пышным
Оживленье ночных похорон:
Льются мрачно-весёлые толпы
Из каких-то божественных недр.

Это солнце ночное хоронит
Возбуждённая играми чернь,
Возвращаясь с полночного пира
Под глухие удары копыт.

И как новый встает Геркуланум,
Спящий город в сияньи луны:
И убогого рынка лачуги,
И могучий дорический ствол.

1918

* * *

When a feverish forum of Moscow
Halts in a warm night, and wide
Throats of the theatres throw
Out the crowds to the squares—

The excitement of night funerals
Streams along sumptuous streets:
Joyously-grim crowds
Flow from some divine depths.

It is mob excited by games,
Returning from a midnight feast,
That buries the night sun
To the dull sound of the hooves.

A sleeping city rises in moonlight
Like a new Herculaneum—both
The huts of a wretched market-place
And a mighty Doric trunk.

1918

* * *

Прославим, братья, сумерки свободы,
Великий сумеречный год!
В кипящие ночные воды
Опущен грузный лес тенёт.
Восходишь ты в глухие годы —
О солнце, судия, народ!

Прославим роковое бремя,
Которое в слезах народный вождь берёт.
Прославим власти сумрачное бремя,
Её невыносимый гнёт.
В ком сердце есть — тот должен слышать, время,
Как твой корабль ко дну идёт.

Мы в легионы боевые
Связали ласточек — и вот
Не видно солнца; вся стихия
Щебечет, движется, живёт;
Сквозь сети — сумерки густые —
Не видно солнца и земля плывёт.

Ну что ж, попробуем: огромный, неуклюжий,
Скрипучий поворот руля.
Земля плывёт. Мужайтесь, мýжи.
Как плугом, океан деля,
Мы будем помнить и в летейской стуже,
Что десяти небес нам стоила земля.

1918, Москва, май

* * *

Hail, brothers, let us praise our freedom's twilight,
The great twilight year!
Into the boiling waters of the night
A heavy forest of snare
Is thrown—into a deadly time
You soar, oh, sun, oh judge, oh, people!

Praise, brothers, the fateful burden
The people's leader takes in tears.
Let's glorify the twilight burden—
The intolerable weight of power.
Whoever has the heart, should hear
Time, how your ship sinks down.

We tied swallows into the fighting legions,
So that the sun grew dark,
While the entire nature
Moves, twitters, lives—creation
Under the snare of a dense dusk—
The sun is dark, and the land sails on.

Well, let us try: a squeaking, huge,
An awkward turn of the wheel.
The land sails on. You, men, take courage!
Plowing through the ocean, we will
Remember that our land cost us ten heavens
Even in a Lethean chill.

Moscow, May 1918

Tristia

Я изучил науку расставанья
В простоволосых жалобах ночных.
Жуют волы, и длится ожиданье,
Последний час вигилий городских.
И чту обряд той петушиной ночи,
Когда, подняв дорожной скорби груз,
Глядели вдаль заплаканные очи
И женский плач мешался с пеньем муз.

Кто может знать при слове — расставанье,
Какая нам разлука предстоит?
Что нам сулит петушье восклицанье,
Когда огонь в акрополе горит?
И на заре какой-то новой жизни,
Когда в сенях лениво вол жует,
Зачем петух, глашатай новой жизни,
На городской стене крылами бьёт?

И я люблю обыкновенье пряжи:
Снуёт челнок, веретено жужжит.
Смотри: навстречу, словно пух лебяжий,
Уже босая Делия летит!
О, нашей жизни скудная основа!
Куда как беден радости язык!
Всё было встарь. Всё повторится снова.
И сладок нам лишь узнаванья миг.

Да будет так: прозрачная фигурка
На чистом блюде глиняном лежит.
Как беличья распластанная шкурка,
Склонясь над воском, девушка глядит.
Не нам гадать о греческом Эребе,
Для женщин воск — что для мужчины медь,
Нам только в битвах выпадает жребий,
А им дано гадая умереть.

1918

Tristia

I have studied the science of parting
In bareheaded nightly woeful moans.
Oxen are chewing and the waiting is lasting
When the last hour of the city vigils goes on.
And I respect the ritual of that rooster night
When lifting up the wanderer's load of woe,
Eyes full of tears looked ahead in fright,
And women's weeping was mixed with the Muses' song.

Who can grasp what separation we'll withstand
When the word "parting" is uttered out loud?
What the rooster's crowing can portend
When the fire in the acropolis is still alight?
And at the dawn of a vague new life,
When the ox is still chewing in the stall,
Why the rooster, the herald of the new life,
Is beating its wings on the city wall?

I too love the routine of weaving:
The spindle buzzes, the shuttle is busy scurrying,
And look: like swan's down in flight
A barefoot Delia takes wing!
Oh, how poor is the warp of our life!
So frugal is the language of delight!
All happened in old days. All will repeat,
And only the trice of recognition is sweet.

So be it thus: a transparent figurine
Lies on a clean earthenware plate.
Like a squirrel's skin spread flat,
Bent over the wax, a girl looks straight.
Greek Erebus is for us unseen,
Wax for women—is as bronze arms for men:
We can draw only in battle our lot,
But they can die foretelling their fate.

1918

* * *

На каменных отрогах Пиэрии
Водили музы первый хоровод,
Чтобы, как пчёлы, лирники слепые
Нам подарили ионийский мёд.
И холодком повеяло высоким
От выпукло-девического лба,
Чтобы раскрылись правнукам далёким
Архипелага нежные гроба.

Бежит весна топтать луга Эллады,
Обула Сафо пёстрый сапожок,
И молоточками куют цикады,
Как в песенке поётся, перстенёк.
Высокий дом построил плотник дюжий,
На свадьбу всех передушили кур,
И растянул сапожник неуклюжий
На башмаки все пять воловьих шкур.

Нерасторопна черепаха-лира,
Едва-едва, беспалая, ползёт.
Лежит себе на солнышке Эпира,
Тихонько грея золотой живот.
Ну, кто её такую приласкает,
Кто спящую её перевернёт —
Она во сне Терпандра ожидает,
Сухих перстов предчувствуя налёт.

Поит дубы холодная криница,
Простоволосая шумит трава,
На радость осам пахнет медуница.
О, где же вы, святые острова,
Где не едят надломленного хлеба,
Где только мёд, вино и молоко,
Скрипучий труд не омрачает неба
И колесо вращается легко.

1919

* * *

On steep stony ridges of Pieria
Muses had their first round of dance,
So that blind lyre-players, like bees,
Would give us the gift of Ionian honey.
Domed brows of maidens breathe
A high feverish cold breeze
So that Archipelago's tender tombs
Would wide open for distant progenies.

Spring rushes to trot the meadows of Hellas,
Sappho has put a pied boot on,
Cicadas forge with their tiny hammers
A tiny signet ring, as sung in a song.
A stalwart carpenter built a high palace,
All chicken were throttled for a wedding feast,
And a sluggish shoemaker spread along
All of his five ox hides beneath.

A tortoise-lyre is heavy, ungainly,
Fingerless, barely crawling, she
Lies in the sun of Epirus and lingers
Warming up her golden belly.
Who would caress such a poor thing,
Who would care to turn her over?
Waiting for a raid of dry fast fingers,
She yearns for Terpander in her dream*.

A cold creek nourishes oak-trees,
Bareheaded grass restlessly rustles,
The wasps delight in lungwort's scent.
Oh, where are you, those holy isles,
Where they don't eat broken bread,
Where there's only honey, milk and wine,
Screechy labor doesn't cloud the skies,
And the turns of the wheel are light.

1919

---

*   Terpander, of Antissa in Lesbos, was a Greek poet and citharede who lived in about the first half of the seventh century BC. He was the father of Greek music and, through it, of lyric poetry, although his own poetical compositions were few and in extremely simple rhythms.

* * *

Сёстры — тяжесть и нежность, одинаковы ваши приметы.
Медуницы и осы тяжёлую розу сосут.
Человек умирает. Песок остывает согретый,
И вчерашнее солнце на чёрных носилках несут.

Ах, тяжёлые соты и нежные сети!
Легче камень поднять, чем имя твоё повторить.
У меня остаётся одна забота на свете:
Золотая забота, как времени бремя избыть.

Словно тёмную воду, я пью помутившийся воздух.
Время вспахано плугом, и роза землёю была.
В медленном водовороте тяжёлые нежные розы,
Розы тяжесть и нежность в двойные венки заплела!

Март 1920 г.

* * *

Sisters—heaviness and tenderness, your traits are akin.
Wasps and honeybees suck at the heavy rose.
Man dies, and hot sand is cooling down,
And a black bier carries away yesterday's sun.

Ah, heavy honeycombs and tender netting!
It is easier to lift up a stone than to utter your name.
In the world I have only one care left, certain,
A golden care how to relieve the burden of time.

Like dark water I drink this turbulent air,
Time is ploughed and a rose was planted in earth.
In a slow whirl, heavy tender roses are
Entwined by the two sisters in a double wreath!

March 1920

* * *

Вернись в смесительное лоно,
Откуда, Лия, ты пришла,
За то, что солнцу Илиона
Ты жёлтый сумрак предпочла.

Иди, никто тебя не тронет,
На грудь отца в глухую ночь
Пускай главу свою уронит
Кровосмесительница-дочь.

Но роковая перемена
В тебе исполниться должна:
Ты будешь Лия — не Елена,
Не потому наречена,

Что царской крови тяжелее
Струиться в жилах, чем другой, —
Нет, ты полюбишь иудея,
Исчезнешь в нём — и Бог с тобой.

1920

* * *

Go back to the incestuous womb,
From where, Leah, you have come,
Because you preferred a yellow twilight
To the bright Ilion's sun.

Go, no one will harm you in your incest,
Let the incestuous daughter in her plight
Drop her head on her father's breast
In the dead of the gloomy night.

But a doomed change in you, unveiling,
Will have to be fulfilled hence:
You will be Leah, not Helen,
You were not named thus since

It is harder for a royal blood than
Any other to stream in the veins,—
No, you will fall in love with a Jew,
And will disappear in him—God be with you!

1920

* * *

Веницейской жизни, мрачной и бесплодной,
Для меня значение светло:
Вот она глядит с улыбкою холодной
В голубое дряхлое стекло.

Тонкий воздух кожи. Синие прожилки.
Белый снег. Зелёная парча.
Всех кладут на кипарисные носилки,
Сонных, тёплых вынимают из плаща.

И горят, горят в корзинах свечи,
Словно голубь залетел в ковчег.
На театре и на праздном вече
Умирает человек.

Ибо нет спасенья от любви и страха:
Тяжелее платины Сатурново кольцо!
Чёрным бархатом завешанная плаха
И прекрасное лицо.

Тяжелы твои, Венеция, уборы,
В кипарисных рамах зеркала.
Воздух твой гранёный. В спальнях тают горы
Голубого дряхлого стекла.

Только в пальцах роза или склянка —
Адриатика зелёная, прости!
Что же ты молчишь, скажи, венецианка,
Как от этой смерти праздничной уйти?

Чёрный Веспер в зеркале мерцает,
Всё проходит. Истина темна.
Человек родится. Жемчуг умирает.
И Сусанна старцев ждать должна.

1920

* * *

The meaning of fruitless and gloomy
Venetian life to me is light.
Here she looks smiling coolly
In the old blue glass' sight.

Blue veins. Skin's delicate air.
White snow. Green brocade's yoke.
Everyone is put onto a cypress bier,
Sleepy and warm, plucked out from one's cloak.

The candles keep burning, burning in the baskets
As if the dove flew back into the Ark.
At the theater and at the assembly banquets
Man dies in light or in dark.

For there's no escape from love and fear:
Heavier than platinum is Saturn's ring!
The executioner's block and a face so fair
Are both in black velvet draped.

Heavy are your attires, Venice,
So are your mirrors in cypress frames.
Your faceted air. A mount of old blue glass
In the bedchamber melts and wanes.

Fingers seize a rose or a flask—
Green Adriatic, forgive me please!
Venetian dame, why are you silent, I ask:
How can one escape this festive death?

Black Vesper flickers in the mirror glass.
Everything passes. Dark truth bewilders.
A man is born. A pearl dies, alas.
And Susanna has to wait for the Elders.

1920

* * *

За то, что я руки твои не сумел удержать,
За то, что я предал солёные нежные губы,
Я должен рассвета в дремучем акрополе ждать —
Как я ненавижу пахучие, древние срубы!

Ахейские мужи во тьме снаряжают коня,
Зубчатыми пилами в стены вгрызаются крепко.
Никак не уляжется крови сухая возня,
И нет для тебя ни названья, ни звука, ни слепка.

Как мог я подумать, что ты возвратишься, как смел?
Зачем преждевременно я от тебя оторвался?
Ещё не рассеялся мрак и петух не пропел,
Ещё в древесину горячий топор не врезался.

Прозрачной слезой на стенах проступила смола,
И чувствует город свои деревянные рёбра,
Но хлынула к лестницам кровь и на приступ пошла,
И трижды приснился мужам соблазнительный образ.

Где милая Троя? Где царский, где девичий дом?
Он будет разрушен, высокий Приамов скворешник.
И падают стрелы сухим деревянным дождём,
И стрелы другие растут на земле, как орешник.

Последней звезды безболезненно гаснет укол,
И серою ласточкой утро в окно постучится,
И медленный день, как в соломе проснувшийся вол,
На стогнах, шершавых от долгого сна, шевелится.

1920

* * *

Because I could not hold your hands in mine,
Because I betrayed your salty tender lips,
I must wait for the dawn in the thick acropolis confines—
How I hate the smell of those ancient wooden forts.

In the darkness Achaeans equip their horse
And rip firmly into the walls their jagged saws.
The dry tumult of blood would never cease,
And there is no name, no sound, no cast of yours.

How did I dare think that you would return?
Why did I leave you, why did I go ahead?
The dark has not scattered and the cock has not crowed yet,
And the blazing ax has not cut the wood in its upturn.

A transparent tear of resin ran down the walls,
And the town feels its wooden ribs, but the blood
Rushed out to the stairs and went on to the assault,
And the men saw a tempting image thrice in their dreams.

Where is sweet Troy, where is the king's, the maidens' house?
It will be destroyed, Priam's high starling nest,
And the dry wooden rain of arrows incessantly pours,
And more arrows grow like a hazel grove from the earth.

A sting of the last star dies out without pain,
And the dawn's gray swallow will knock on the window pane,
And a slow day like an ox in the straw wakes up
Stirring on the rugged squares after a long sleep.

1920

Из книги «Стихотворения»
(1928 г., стихотворения 1921–1925 гг.)

* * *

С розовой пеной усталости у мягких губ
Яростно волны зелёные роет бык,
Фыркает, гребли не любит — женолюб,
Ноша хребту непривычна, и труд велик.

Изредка выскочит дельфина колесо
Да повстречается морской колючий ёж.
Нежные руки Европы, берите всё!
Где ты для выи желанней ярмо найдёшь?

Горько внимает Европа могучий плеск,
Тучное море кругом закипает в ключ,
Видно, страшит её вод маслянистых блеск
И соскользнуть бы хотелось с шершавых круч.

О, сколько раз ей милее уключин скрип,
Лоном широкая палуба, гурт овец
И за высокой кормою мельканье рыб!
С нею безве́сельный дальше плывёт гребец.

1922

From *Poems*
(1928, poems of 1921–1925)

---

* * *

With the pink foam of fatigue around soft lips,
Furiously a bull plows green waves,
He dislikes rowing, a womanizer, he snorts,
Labor is hard, and his back is not used to a hefty weight.

Rarely a wheel of a dolphin would jump out
Or a prickly sea hedgehog would come across.
Europe's tender hands, its all yours!
Where would one find a better yoke for a neck?

Bitterly Europe listens to a mighty splash,
A fat sea around boils and raves,
She seems to fear an oily blaze
Or else she would glide from these rough slopes.

Oh, how much sweeter for her is the rowlocks' squeak,
A herd of sheep and a wide womb of a deck,
And the flashing of fish behind a high stern!
But an oarless rower swims on with her on his back.

1922

Век

Век мой, зверь мой, кто сумеет
Заглянуть в твои зрачки
И своею кровью склеит
Двух столетий позвонки?
Кровь-строительница хлещет
Горлом из земных вещей,
Захребетник лишь трепещет
На пороге новых дней.

Тварь, покуда жизнь хватает,
Донести хребет должна,
И невидимым играет
Позвоночником волна.
Словно нежный хрящ ребёнка
Век младенческой земли.
Снова в жертву, как ягнёнка,
Темя жизни принесли.

Чтобы вырвать век из плена,
Чтобы новый мир начать,
Узловатых дней колена
Нужно флейтою связать.
Это век волну колышет
Человеческой тоской,
И в траве гадюка дышит
Мерой века золотой.

И ещё набухнут почки,
Брызнет зелени побег,
Но разбит твой позвоночник,
Мой прекрасный жалкий век!
И с бессмысленной улыбкой
Вспять глядишь, жесток и слаб,
Словно зверь, когда-то гибкий,
На следы своих же лап.

The Age

My age, my beast, who can try
Look straight into your eye
And weld with one's own blood
The vertebrae of two centuries?
A stream of building blood pours
From the throat of earthly things,
Only a sluggard without a backbone
Trembles on the brink of new days.

A creature, while still alive,
Should carry its spine on,
And the wave plays
With an unseen backbone.
Infantile age of earth
Is like tender baby's bones—
The life's crown again
Is sacrificed like a lamb.

To tear the age from bounds,
To start a new world,
The knotty joints of days
Should be bound by the flute sounds.
The age sways waves
With a human angst that stings,
While the adder breathes in the grass
With a golden measure of things.

The buds will burst and the grass,
And a green shoot will surge,
But your backbone is broken, alas,
My wonderful wretched age!
A cruel and weak beast,
You gaze with a senseless smile
At the trails of your own paws,
Like a beast once strong and agile.

*Исключенная строфа:**

Кровь-строительница хлещет
Горлом из земных вещей,
И горячей рыбой плещет
В берег тёплый хрящ морей.
И с высокой сетки птичьей,
От лазурных влажных глыб
Льётся, льётся безразличье
На смертельный твой ушиб.

1922

---

* Как указано в комментариях А. Г. Меца (Полное собрание сочинений и писем,
т. 1., с. 581), в журнале «Красная новь» (1923, № 1) текст стихотворения был
опубликован с ошибочно повторенным текстом предшествующей строфы
в ст. 21–24. Так как большинство переводчиков этого стихотворения приводят
перевод этой строфы, здесь он также приводится в качестве приложения.

*Excluded stanza:**

Streams of building blood pour
From the throat of earthly things,
And a warm cartilage of the seas
Sways searing fish ashore,
And from the bird's height,
From azure wet rocks
Indifference flows down
Upon your mortal wound, beast.

1922

---

*   It is noted by A. G. Mets (Mandel'shtam, *Polnoe sobraniie sochinenii i pisem*, 1:581) that in
the publication of this poem in the magazine *Krasnaia nov'* [Red news] 1 (1923), the lines
of the previous stanza (21–24) were repeated by mistake. Since most of the translators of
this poem into English included this stanza, it is also published here as an addition.

Нашедший подкову
(Пиндарический отрывок)

Глядим на лес и говорим:
Вот лес корабельный, мачтовый,
Розовые сосны,
До самой верхушки свободные от мохнатой ноши,
Им бы поскрипывать в бурю,
Одинокими пиниями,
В разъярённом безлесном воздухе.
Под солёною пятою ветра устоит отвес,
                                        пригнанный к пляшущей палубе,
И мореплаватель,
В необузданной жажде пространства,
Влача через влажные рытвины хрупкий прибор геометра,
Сличит с притяженьем земного лона
Шероховатую поверхность морей.

А вдыхая запах
Смолистых слёз, проступивших сквозь обшивку корабля,
Любуясь на доски,
Заклёпанные, слаженные в переборки
Не вифлеемским мирным плотником, а другим —
Отцом путешествий, другом морехода, —
Говорим:
И они стояли на земле,
Неудобной, как хребет осла,
Забывая верхушками о корнях,
На знаменитом горном кряже,
И шумели под пресным ливнем,
Безуспешно предлагая небу выменять на щепотку соли
Свой благородный груз.

С чего начать?
Всё трещит и качается.
Воздух дрожит от сравнений.
Ни одно слово не лучше другого,
Земля гудит метафорой,
И лёгкие двуколки

The Horseshoe Finder
(A Pindaric fragment)

We look at a forest and say:
Here is timber for ships and masts,
Rosy pines,
Free of hairy burden to their very tops,
They should screech in the storm
As lonely pines
In a raging forestless air.
The plumb-line fastened firmly to the dancing deck will endure
                            a salty sole of the wind,

And a seafarer,
In his untamed thirst for space
Drags through soggy furrows a fragile instrument of a geometer
To weigh a rugged surface of the seas
Against the attraction of the terrestrial bosom.

Inhaling the scent
Of tarry tears which exude through plaiting,
Admiring the clamped planks of bulkheads
Which were not riveted by a Bethlehem's peaceful carpenter,
                            but by another,
The father of sea-fares, the friend of a seafarer,
We say:
They too stood on land
Uncomfortable as a mule's backbone,
Their tops were forgetting about the roots
In a famous mountainous ridge,
And rustling under a freshwater torrents,
They offered heaven in vain to trade their noble load
For a pinch of salt.

Where to start?
Everything cracks and sways.
The air trembles with similes.
No word is better than any other,
The earth drones with metaphors,
And light two-wheeled chariots,

В броской упряжи густых от натуги птичьих стай
Разрываются на части,
Соперничая с храпящими любимцами ристалищ.

Трижды блажен, кто введёт в песнь имя;
Украшенная названьем песнь
Дольше живёт среди других —
Она отмечена среди подруг повязкой на лбу,
Исцеляющей от беспамятства, слишком сильного
                                 одуряющего запаха,
Будь то близость мужчины,
Или запах шерсти сильного зверя,
Или просто дух чобра, растёртого между ладоней.

Воздух бывает тёмным, как вода, и всё живое в нём плавает, как рыба,
Плавниками расталкивая сферу,
Плотную, упругую, чуть нагретую, —
Хрусталь, в котором движутся колёса и шарахаются лошади,
Влажный чернозём Нееры, каждую ночь распаханный заново
Вилами, трезубцами, мотыгами, плугами.
Воздух замешан так же густо, как земля:
Из него нельзя выйти, в него трудно войти.

Шорох пробегает по деревьям зелёной лаптой.
Дети играют в бабки позвонками умерших животных.
Хрупкое летоисчисление нашей эры подходит к концу.
Спасибо за то, что было:
Я сам ошибся, я сбился, запутался в счёте.
Эра звенела, как шар золотой,
Полая, литая, никем не поддерживаемая,
На всякое прикосновение отвечала «да» и «нет».
Так ребенок отвечает:
«Я дам тебе яблоко» или: «Я не дам тебе яблока»,
И лицо его точный слепок с голоса, который произносит эти слова.

Звук ещё звенит, хотя причина звука исчезла.
Конь лежит в пыли и храпит в мыле,
Но крутой поворот его шеи
Ещё сохраняет воспоминание о беге с разбросанными ногами —

Dazzlingly harnessed to flocks of birds strenuously flapping their wings,
Fall to fragments
Competing with snorting favorites of the races.

Thrice-blessed is he who puts a name in a song;
A song embossed with a name
Outlives the others—
It is set apart from her girlfriends by a headband,
Healing from oblivion by a befuddling odor too strong
                                        to endure,
Whether caused by the imminence of a man
Or the smell of a strong beast's fur,
Or just by the scent of thyme grated in the palms.

The air can be as dark as water, and all creatures swim in it like fish
Whose fins thrust the sphere,
Dense, pliable, slightly warmed—
A crystal, where wheels revolve and horses shy,
A soggy black soil of Neaera each night plowed anew
By pitchforks, tridents, hoes, ploughs.
The air is kneaded as densely as soil—
It is impossible to leave it, hard to enter.

A rustle rushes through the trees like a green bat,
Children play knucklebones with the vertebrae of extinct beasts,
The frail chronology of our era comes to a close.
I am grateful for what was given:
I myself was lost, made blunders, lost count.
The era was ringing like a golden orb,
Hollow, cast, supported by no one,
Responding "Yes" or "No" to each touch,
Thus a child answers:
"I'll give you an apple" or: "I won't give you an apple,"
While his face is an exact cast of his voice, which utters those words.

The sound is still ringing although its source has vanished.
The steed lies in the dust and snorts dripping with sweat,
But a steep turn of its neck
Still keeps the memory of a thrush-legged race—

Когда их было не четыре,
А по числу камней дороги,
Обновляемых в четыре смены,
По числу отталкиваний от земли
        пышущего жаром иноходца.

Так
Нашедший подкову
Сдувает с неё пыль
И растирает её шерстью, пока она не заблестит.
Тогда
Он вешает её на пороге,
Чтобы она отдохнула,
И больше уж ей не придётся высекать искры из кремня.
Человеческие губы,
        которым больше нечего сказать,
Сохраняют форму последнего сказанного слова,
И в руке остаётся ощущение тяжести,
Хотя кувшин
    наполовину расплескался,
        пока его несли домой.

То, что я сейчас говорю, говорю не я,
А вырыто из земли, подобно зёрнам окаменелой пшеницы.
Одни на монетах изображают льва,
Другие — голову.
Разнообразные медные, золотые и бронзовые лепёшки
С одинаковой почестью лежат в земле,
Век, пробуя их перегрызть, оттиснул на них свои зубы.
Время срезает меня, как монету,
И мне уж не хватает меня самого.

1923, Москва

Not a four-hoofed race,
But as many hooves as there were cobblestones
Renewed in four shifts
As many times as a steed foaming with
Heat hit the ground.

Thus
The horseshoe-finder
Blows the dust off it
And polishes it with wool until it shines.
Then
He hangs it on his doorway
Giving it rest,
So it won't have to strike sparks from flint.
Human lips
               which have nothing more to say
Keep the form of the last uttered word,
And a feeling of heaviness fills the hand
Though the jug
    has been half-spilled
                  while it was carried home.

What I am saying now is not spoken by me
But is dug out like grains of petrified wheat.
Some stamp lions on coins,
Others, a head.
Various copper, bronze and golden lozenges
Are buried in earth with equal honor.
The age has tried to gnaw at them leaving the clench of its teeth.
Time cuts me like a coin,
And there is not enough of my self left for myself.

1923, Moscow

Грифельная ода

Звезда с звездой — могучий стык,
Кремнистый путь из старой песни,
Кремня и воздуха язык,
Кремень с водой, с подковой перстень,
На мягком сланце облаков
Молочный грифельный рисунок —
Не ученичество миров,
А бред овечьих полусонок.

Мы стоя спим в густой ночи
Под тёплой шапкою овечьей.
Обратно в крепь родник журчит
Цепочкой, пеночкой и речью.
Здесь пишет страх, здесь пишет сдвиг
Свинцовой палочкой молочной,
Здесь созревает черновик
Учеников воды проточной.

Крутые козьи города,
Кремней могучее слоенье,
И всё-таки ещё гряда —
Овечьи церкви и селенья!
Им проповедует отвес,
Вода их учит, точит время —
И воздуха прозрачный лес
Уже давно пресыщен всеми.

Как мёртвый шершень возле сот,
День пёстрый выметен с позором.
И ночь-коршунница несёт
Горящий мел и грифель кормит.
С иконоборческой доски
Стереть дневные впечатленья
И, как птенца, стряхнуть с руки
Уже прозрачные виденья!

The Slate Ode

A star with a star is a mighty joint,
A flinty way from the old song,
The tongue of air and flint,
Flint with water, a horseshoe ring.
A milky slate-sketch is drawn
On a soft schist of the clouds—
Not the apprenticeship of the worlds,
But hallucinations of sheep's dream.

We sleep on foot under a dense night,
Beneath a warm sheepskin hat.
A stream babbles back to its source,
Like a foamy warbler, a chain, a speech.
Here terror writes, here a shift writes
With a leaden milky stick,
Here a draft grows ripe
Of the flowing water's disciples.

Steep goatish towns,
A mighty layering of flint,
Yet, there's another ridge on height—
Sheepish villages and churches!
There a plumb-line preaches,
Time gnaws, water teaches,
And a transparent wood of air
Has had a surfeit of them all.

Like a dead hornet from a hive,
A pied day is swept off with disgrace;
A hawkish night carries a burning chalk
And feeds the slate to erase
A day's impressions away
From the iconoclastic board
And shake off transparent visions
Like nestlings from the hand!

Плод нарывал. Зрел виноград.
День бушевал, как день бушует.
И в бабки нежная игра,
И в полдень злых овчарок шубы;
Как мусор с ледяных высот —
Изнанка образов зелёных —
Вода голодная течёт,
Крутясь, играя, как звёреныш.

И как паук ползет ко мне —
Где каждый стык луной обрызган,
На изумлённой крутизне
Я слышу грифельные визги.
Твои ли, память, голоса
Учительствуют, ночь ломая,
Бросая грифели лесам,
Из птичьих клювов вырывая?

Мы только с голоса поймём,
Что там царапалось, боролось,
И чёрствый грифель поведём
Туда, куда укажет голос.
Ломаю ночь, горящий мел
Для твёрдой записи мгновенной.
Меняю шум на пенье стрел,
Меняю строй на стрепет гневный.

Кто я? Не каменщик прямой,
Не кровельщик, не корабельщик —
Двурушник я, с двойной душой,
Я ночи друг, я дня застрельщик.
Блажен, кто называл кремень
Учеником воды проточной!
Блажен, кто завязал ремень
Подошве гор на твёрдой почве!

The fruit was swelling. The grapes grew ripe.
The day was raging like most days.
A tender game of knucklebones first,
The furs of fierce sheepdogs at noon.
The underside of green images
Is like dross of the icy heights—
The hungry water flows and spins,
And plays like a cub of a wild beast.

And like a spider crawls up to me—
Here each joint is drenched in moonlight,
I hear shrieks across the slate board
On the astonished steep height.
Are those, memory, your voices
Teaching me—they break the night,
Throwing slate pencils to the woods,
Snatching them out from the birds' beaks?

It is only by the voice we'll know
What scribbled and struggled there
And lead a stiff lead pencil where
The voice will lead us and will show.
I break the night, a burning chalk,
To make a steadfast instant note,
I trade the noise for the arrows' song,
I trade harmony for a strembling wrath.

Who am I? I am not a straight stonemason,
Neither a shipbuilder, nor a roofer—
I am a double-dealer, with a double soul,
A friend of night and a daymonger.
Blessed is he who called flint
A disciple of the flowing water,
Blessed is he who tied the strap
Of the mountains' foot on solid soil!

И я теперь учу дневник
Царапин грифельного лета,
Кремня и воздуха язык,
С прослойкой тьмы, с прослойкой света,
И я хочу вложить персты
В кремнистый путь из старой песни,
Как в язву, заключая встык —
Кремень с водой, с подковой перстень.

1923

So, now I study the record
Of the slate summer scratches,
The language of flint and air,
With a layer of darkness, a layer of light,
And I yearn to put my fingers
In the flinty way from the old song
As in a sore—to weld and join
Flint with water, a horseshoe with a ring.

1923

* * *

Язык булыжника мне голубя понятней,
Здесь камни — голуби, дома — как голубятни,
И светлым ручейком течёт рассказ подков
По звучным мостовым прабабки городов.
Здесь толпы детские — событий попрошайки,
Парижских воробьев испуганные стайки —
Клевали наскоро крупу свинцовых крох,
Фригийской бабушкой рассыпанный горох…
И в воздухе плывёт забытая коринка,
И в памяти живёт плетёная корзинка,
И тесные дома — зубов молочных ряд
На дёснах старческих — как близнецы стоят.

Здесь клички месяцам давали, как котятам,
И молоко и кровь давали нежным львятам,
А подрастут они — то разве года два
Держалась на плечах большая голова!
Большеголовые — там руки поднимали
И клятвой на песке как яблоком играли.
Мне трудно говорить: не видел ничего,
Но всё-таки скажу: я помню одного;
Он лапу поднимал, как огненную розу,
И, как ребёнок, всем показывал занозу.
Его не слушали: смеялись кучера,
И грызла яблоки, с шарманкой, детвора.
Афиши клеили, и ставили капканы,
И пели песенки, и жарили каштаны,
И светлой улицей, как просекой прямой,
Летели лошади из зелени густой!

1923

* * *

Clearer than pigeon's talk to me is stone's tongue,
Here stones are doves, and houses are like dovecotes.
The horseshoes' tale runs like a bright stream along
The ringing cobbles of the great grandmother of all towns.
Here crowds of children begged for the events and shows,
While frightened flocks of Paris sparrows
Hurriedly pecked cereals of leaden crumbs—
Peas scattered by the Phrygian granny...
Forgotten currants are floating in the air,
My memory keeps plaited baskets alive,
And cramped houses—a row of baby teeth
In the old gums like twins stand there.

Here they named months like kittens
And raised tender lion cubs on milk and blood;
When they grew, the neck would hold
A big lion's head for two years at best!
The bigheaded there raised their hands and,
Like an apple, played with an oath on sand.
It's hard to say—I did not see a thing,
Yet I will say, remembering one of them:
He raised his paw like a burning rose
And like a child showed a thorn to those
Who would not listen: coachmen grinned,
Kids crunched apples to the barrel organ's tune,
They glued posters and put up traps,
Sang songs, fried chestnuts, and soon
The horses rushed from a dark green
Along a bright street, as through a straight lane!

1923

А небо будущим беременно . . .

Опять войны разноголосица
На древних плоскогорьях мира,
И лопастью пропеллер лоснится,
Как кость точёная тапира.
Крыла и смерти уравнение
С алгебраических пирушек,
Слетев, он помнит измерение
Других эбеновых игрушек,
Врагиню-ночь, рассадник вражеский
Существ коротких ластоногих,
И молодую силу тяжести:
Так начиналась власть немногих...

Итак, готовьтесь жить во времени,
Где нет ни волка, ни тапира,
А небо будущим беременно —
Пшеницей сытого эфира.
А то сегодня победители
Кладбища лёта обходили,
Ломали крылья стрекозиные
И молоточками казнили.

Давайте слушать грома проповедь,
Как внуки Себастьяна Баха,
И на востоке и на западе
Органные поставим крылья!
Давайте бросим бури яблоко
На стол пирующим землянам
И на стеклянном блюде облако
Поставим яств посередине.

Давайте всё покроем заново
Камчатной скатертью пространства,
Переговариваясь, радуясь,
Друг другу подавая брашна.

And the Sky is Pregnant with the Future . . .

Again, war's many-voiced dissonance
Reigns on the world's ancient plateaus,
And the propeller's blade glades
Like the tapered bone of a tapir.
The wing-and-death equation
From algebraic feasts: descending,
He remembers dimensions
Of the other ebony playthings:
The enemy-night, a hostile breeder
Of short pinniped creatures,
And a young force of heaviness—
Thus, the power of the few commenced...

So be ready to live in times
Where there's neither a wolf nor a tapir,
And the sky is pregnant with the future—
Of the ether replete with wheat.
Or else today the winners
Walking around the flight's graveyards,
Crushed the wings of the dragonflies
And slayed them with little hammers.

Let's listen to the thunder's sermon,
Like Sebastian Bach's grandsons,
Both in the East and in the West
We'll put up the wings of organs!
Let's throw the tempest's apple
On the table of feasting earthlings,
And put a cloud on a glassy platter
In the middle of their banquets.

Let's cover everything anew
With a Damask tablecloth of space,
Talking and enjoying one another,
Passing each other the viands.

На круговом, на мирном судьбище
Зарёю кровь оледенится,
В беременном глубоком будущем
Жужжит большая медуница.

А вам, в безвременьи летающим
Под хлыст войны за власть немногих, —
Хотя бы честь млекопитающих,
Хотя бы совесть — ластоногих.
И тем печальнее, тем горше нам,
Что люди-птицы хуже зверя,
И что стервятникам и коршунам
Мы поневоле больше верим.
Как шапка холода альпийского,
Из году в год, в жару и лето,
На лбу высоком человечества
Войны холодные ладони.
А ты, глубокое и сытое,
Забременевшее лазурью,
Как чешуя, многоочитое,
И альфа и омега бури, —
Тебе — чужое и безбровое —
Из поколенья в поколение
Всегда высокое и новое
Передается удивление.

1923, 1929

On the round and peaceful trial
The dawn will freeze the blood,
And a big honey bee is humming
In a pregnant deep future.

And you, flying in lost times,
Whipped by the war, for the rule of the few,
Should have at least the dignity of the mammals
Or the consciousness—of the pinnipeds.
The more sorrowful the bitterer we are
That human birds are worse than beasts,
And against our will we trust more
Hawks and vultures these days.
The war's cold hands
Year after year, in summer's heat
Are like a hat of the Alpine's cold
On the high brow of humankind.
And to you, deep and fullfed,
Pregnant with azure sky,
Like fish scale, many-eyed,
The tempest's alpha and omega,
To you—lacking eyebrows and alien—
From generation to generation
Surprise and wonder are conveyed
Always new and high.

1923, 1929

1 января 1924

Кто время целовал в измученное темя —
С сыновьей нежностью потом
Он будет вспоминать, как спать ложилось время
В сугроб пшеничный за окном.
Кто веку поднимал болезненные веки —
Два сонных яблока больших, —
Он слышит вечно шум, когда взревели реки
Времён обманных и глухих.

Два сонных яблока у века-властелина
И глиняный прекрасный рот,
Но к млеющей руке стареющего сына
Он, умирая, припадёт.
Я знаю, с каждым днём слабеет жизни выдох,
Ещё немного — оборвут
Простую песенку о глиняных обидах
И губы оловом зальют.

О, глиняная жизнь! О, умиранье века!
Боюсь, лишь тот поймёт тебя,
В ком беспомóщная улыбка человека,
Который потерял себя.
Какая боль — искать потерянное слово,
Больные веки поднимать
И с известью в крови для племени чужого
Ночные травы собирать.

Век. Известковый слой в крови больного сына
Твердеет. Спит Москва, как деревянный ларь,
И некуда бежать от века-властелина . . .
Снег пахнет яблоком, как встарь.
Мне хочется бежать от моего порога.
Куда? На улице темно,
И, словно сыплют соль мощёною дорогой,
Белеет совесть предо мной.

January 1, 1924

He who kissed time's tormented temples,
With a son's tenderness will recollect
How time lay down to sleep
Behind the window in a snowy mount of wheat.
He who raised time's sickly eyelids—
Two enormous sleepy apples—
Will always hear the noise of roaring rivers
Of deceptive and deadly times.

A tyrannous age has two sleepy apples
And a beautiful mouth of clay,
But on his death-bed he will grapple
A drooping hand of his aging son.
I know that life's breath wanes day by day,
They will cut off soon
A simple song of clay wrongs
And seal the mouth with tin.

Oh, life of clay! Oh, dying age!
I fear the only one who can
Grasp you is he whose helpless smile
Reveals a man who lost himself.
It's such a pain to look for a lost word,
To raise sickly eyelids, and when
One's blood is thickened with quicklime,
To gather night herbs for a foreign tribe.

The age. The layer of lime thickens in sick son's blood.
Moscow sleeps like a wooden chest.
There is nowhere to run from a tyrannous age . . .
Like in old days, the snow smells of apples.
I crave to run away from my own porch.
Where to? It's dark outside,
And as if a paved road sprinkled with salt,
My consciousness ahead is shining white.

По переулочкам, скворешням и застрехам,
Недалеко, собравшись как-нибудь, —
Я, рядовой седок, укрывшись рыбьим мехом,
Всё силюсь полость застегнуть.
Мелькает улица, другая,
И яблоком хрустит саней морозный звук,
Не поддаётся петелька тугая,
Всё время валится из рук.

Каким железным, скобяным товаром
Ночь зимняя гремит по улицам Москвы,
То мёрзлой рыбою стучит, то хлещет паром
Из чайных розовых, как серебром плотвы.
Москва — опять Москва. Я говорю ей: «Здравствуй!
Не обессудь, теперь уж не беда,
По старине я принимаю братство
Мороза крепкого и щучьего суда».

Пылает на снегу аптечная малина,
И где-то щёлкнул ундервуд;
Спина извозчика и снег на пол-аршина:
Чего тебе ещё? Не тронут, не убьют.
Зима-красавица, и в звёздах небо козье
Рассыпалось и молоком горит,
И конским волосом о мёрзлые полозья
Вся полость трётся и звенит.

А переулочки коптили керосинкой,
Глотали снег, малину, лёд.
Всё шелушится им советской сонатинкой,
Двадцатый вспоминая год.
Ужели я предам позорному злословью —
Вновь пахнет яблоком мороз —

Past lanes, past starling houses, wooden eaves,
Somehow going somewhere not too far,
A regular rider covered in a threadbare fur,
I try to button up sleigh's robe.
Street after street runs past,
Sleigh's frozen sound crunches like an apple,
A tight loop would not give up and keeps
Slipping out of my hands so hard to grapple.

With what iron hardware does winter night
Jingle along Moscow streets?
It rattles with frozen fish, streams steam
Like silver roach-fish from rosy tearooms.
Moscow—it's Moscow again. I say "Hello!
Bear with me—let bygones be bygones,
As in old time, I respect the brotherhood
Of hard frost and pike's court."*

Pharmacist's raspberry burns in the snow,
An Underwood somewhere clinks;
Two feet of snow and a coachman's back:
What else to wish? You won't be hurt or killed.
Winter's a beauty, and a goat-like starlit sky
Scattered around is burning like milk;
With a horse's hair against the frozen runners
The sleigh's robe rubs and rings.

The lanes smoked with kerosene,
Swallowed snow, raspberry, ice,
Remembering the year of twenty and nineteen,
Scaling off the Soviet sonatina like dry fish.
Can I betray to a shameful smear—
The frost smells of apples again—

---

*   An allusion to the satirical fable "Carp-Idealist" by the great Russian satirist Mikhail
Saltykov-Shchedrin (1826–1889). In the story, Carp was proclaiming ideas of equality,
observing the laws, which were labeled as "socialist," and in the end, called for a dispute
with Pike, was later taken in custody, and finally eaten, or, rather, occasionally swallowed
by Pike.

Присягу чудную четвёртому сословью
И клятвы крупные до слёз?

Кого ещё убьешь? Кого ещё прославишь?
Какую выдумаешь ложь?
То ундервуда хрящ: скорее вырви клавиш —
И щучью косточку найдёшь;
И известковый слой в крови больного сына
Растает, и блаженный брызнет смех…
Но пишущих машин простая сонатина —
Лишь тень сонат могучих тех.

1924

The wonderful oath to the fourth estate*
And the wows as great as tears?

Whom else will you kill? Whom will you hail?
What lies will you devise?
That's the Underwood's cartilage—tear out a key,
And you'll find a pike's bone underneath;
And the layer of quicklime in the blood of a sick son
Will dissolve, and a blessed laughter will burst . . .
But the typewriters' simple sonatina is just
A shadow of those mighty sonatas to come.

1924

* See note 89 on p. 48.

* * *

Нет, никогда, ничей я не был современник,
Мне не с руки почёт такой.
О, как противен мне какой-то соименник —
То был не я, то был другой.

Два сонных яблока у века-властелина
И глиняный прекрасный рот,
Но к млеющей руке стареющего сына
Он, умирая, припадёт.

Я с веком поднимал болезненные веки —
Два сонных яблока больших,
И мне гремучие рассказывали реки
Ход воспалённых тяжб людских.

Сто лет тому назад подушками белела
Складная лёгкая постель,
И странно вытянулось глиняное тело —
Кончался века первый хмель.

Среди скрипучего похода мирового —
Какая лёгкая кровать!
Ну что же, если нам не выковать другого,
Давайте с веком вековать.

И в жаркой комнате, в кибитке и в палатке
Век умирает, а потом —
Два сонных яблока на роговой облатке
Сияют перистым огнём!

1924

* * *

No, I've never been anyone's contemporary—
Such an honor is not for me,
How disgusting is a namesake, unnecessary,—
That was not me, it was he.

A tyrannous age has two sleepy apples
And a beautiful mouth of clay,
But on his death-bed he will grapple
The drooping hand of his aging son.

I raised my sickly eyelids with the age—
Two enormous sleepy apples,
And rattling rivers told me in rage
About the fevered lawsuits of the people.

A folded light bed was an age ago
White with pillows like snow,
But a clay body strangely stretched along—
The first inebriation of the age was gone.

Amid a squeaky world's march—
Such a light-feathered bed!
Well, if we can't forge another age,
Let's live out our lives with it.

In a hot room, in a wagon, in a tent
The age is dying, and then—
Two sleepy apples on a corneous wafer
Shine with a feather-like flame!

1924

* * *

Я буду метаться по табору улицы тёмной
За веткой черёмухи в чёрной рессорной карете,
За капором снега, за вечным, за мельничным шумом.

Я только запомнил каштановых прядей осечки,
Придымленных горечью — нет, с муравьиной кислинкой;
От них на губах остаётся янтарная сухость.

В такие минуты и воздух мне кажется карим,
И кольца зрачков одеваются выпушкой светлой;
И то, что я знаю о яблочной, розовой коже . . .

Но всё же скрипели извозчичьих санок полозья,
В плетёнку рогожи глядели колючие звёзды,
И били вразрядку копыта по клавишам мёрзлым.

И только и свету, что в звёздной колючей неправде!
А жизнь проплывёт театрального капора пеной,
И некому молвить: «Из табора улицы тёмной . . .»

Весна 1925

* * *

I'll rush along a gypsy camp of a dark street
In a black spring carriage chasing a bird cherry branch,
A hood of snow, an eternal noise of the mill . . .

I only remember the misfire of auburn locks,
Smoked with bitterness—no, with a touch of ant's acid
That leaves amber dryness on the lips.

In such moments the air seems brown
And eye rings are covered with a light edging;
And all that I learned about a rosy-apple skin . . .

Yet the sledges of sleighs slightly screeched,
And prickly stars looked down at the wicker rag
While the hooves struck with intervals at the frozen keys.

The only light is that of starry prickly untruth!
And life will float by as the foam of a theater bonnet,
But there's no one to say: "From a gypsy camp of a dark street . . ."

Spring 1925

Из Новых стихотворений
1930–1934 гг.

Армения

> Как бык шестикрылый и грозный
> Здесь людям является труд,
> И, кровью набухнув венозной,
> Предзимние розы цветут.

1

Ты розу Гафиза колышешь
И нянчишь зверушек-детей,
Плечьми осьмигранными дышишь
Мужицких бычачьих церквей.

Окрашена охрою хриплой,
Ты вся далеко за горой,
А здесь лишь картинка налипла
Из чайного блюдца с водой.

From *New Poems*
of 1930–1934

Armenia

> Like a six-winged fearful bull
> Here labor appears to people,
> And swollen with venous blood,
> Midwinter roses bloom.

1

You rock the rose of Hafiz,
You nurse your babies like beasts,
You breathe with the octagonal shoulders
Of rough peasant bull churches.

Painted with a hoarse ochre tincture,
You are all far behind the great mount,
And here is just a decal picture
Stuck to a tea-saucer with water.

2

Ах, ничего я не вижу, и бедное ухо оглохло,
Всех-то цветов мне осталось — лишь сурик да хриплая охра.

И почему-то мне начало утро армянское сниться,
Думал — возьму посмотрю, как живёт в Эривани синица,

Как нагибается булочник, с хлебом играющий в жмурки,
Из очага вынимает лавашные влажные шкурки . . .

Ах, Эривань, Эривань! Иль птица тебя рисовала,
Или раскрашивал лев, как дитя, из цветного пенала?

Ах, Эривань, Эривань! Не город — орешек калёный,
Улиц твоих большеротых кривые люблю вавилоны.

Я бестолковую жизнь, как мулла свой коран, замусолил,
Время свое заморозил и крови горячей не пролил.

Ах, Эривань, Эривань, ничего мне больше не надо,
Я не хочу твоего замороженного винограда!

21 октября 1930

2

Ah, I can't see a thing, and my poor ear is deaf,
Of all colors, I am left red lead and hoarse ochre.

All of a sudden, I started to dream of the Armenian morning,
Going to see how a blue tit in Yerevan is doing,

How a baker bends playing hide-and-seek with bread,
Taking out wet hides of pita lavash from the oven's bed . . .

Ah, Yerevan, Yerevan! Has a bird painted you or
A lion like a child with pencils from a colored case?

Ah, Yerevan, Yerevan! Not a city—a roasted nutlet,
I like the curved Babylons of your big-mouthed streets.

I read my confused life to tatters, like a mullah his Koran,
I froze my time and did not shed my hot blood.

Ah, Yerevan, Yerevan! I don't need a thing,
I don't want your frozen grapes anymore!

October 21, 1930

3

Ты красок себе пожелала —
И выхватил лапой своей
Рисующий лев из пенала
С полдюжины карандашей.

Страна москательных пожаров
И мёртвых гончарных равнин,
Ты рыжебородых сардаров
Терпела средь камней и глин.

Вдали якорей и трезубцев,
Где жухлый почил материк,
Ты видела всех жизнелюбцев,
Всех казнелюбивых владык.

И, крови моей не волнуя,
Как детский рисунок просты,
Здесь жёны проходят, даруя
От львиной своей красоты.

Как люб мне язык твой зловещий,
Твои молодые гроба,
Где буквы — кузнечные клещи
И каждое слово — скоба . . .

26 октября — 16 ноября 1930

3

You wished colors—and then
A lion-artist's paw at once
Snatched out half a dozen
Colorful pencils from a case.

The land of dry-salter fires
And dead pottery plains,
You endured red-bearded Sardars
Amid rocks and clay.

Far from the anchors and tridents,
Where a withered dead continent lies,
You saw all torture-loving tyrants,
All those lovers of life.

Women here pass by bestowing
Upon me their lioness beauty,
Simple as a child's drawing,
They never disturb my blood.

How dear is your ominous tongue,
Your coffins are rough and young,
Where the letters are blacksmith's tongs,
And each word is as hard as a crampon . . .

October 26–November 16, 1930

4

Закутав рот, как влажную розу,
Держа в руках осьмигранные соты,
Всё утро дней на окраине мира
Ты простояла, глотая слёзы.

И отвернулась со стыдом и скорбью
От городов бородатых Востока —
И вот лежишь на москательном ложе,
И с тебя снимают посмертную маску.

25 октября 1930

5

Руку платком обмотай и в венценосный шиповник,
В самую гущу его целлулоидных терний,
Смело, до хруста, её погрузи . . . Добудем розу без ножниц!
Но смотри, чтобы он не осыпался сразу —
Розовый мусор — муслин — лепесток соломоновый —
И для шербета негодный дичок, не дающий ни масла, ни запаха.

4

Covering your mouth like a dewy rose,
Holding octagonal honeycombs in your hands,
You stood swallowing tears the whole morning
Of the days in the world's outskirts.

And you turned away with shame and sorrow
From the bearded towns of the East,
And now you lie on a dry-salter deathbed,
And they cast your death mask.

October 25, 1930

5

Wrap your hand in a handkerchief and boldly
Plunge it, till it cracks, in the depth of a royal wild rose,
Into its celluloid thorns . . . Let's get a rose without scissors!
Yet watch lest the petals at once fall down—
A pinky dross—muslin—a salmon petal of Solomon—
A wilding useless for sherbet, without any scent or oil.

6

Орущих камней государство —
                Армения, Армения!
Хриплые горы к оружью зовущая —
                Армения, Армения!

К трубам серебряным Азии вечно летящая —
                Армения, Армения!
Солнца персидские деньги щедро раздаривающая —
                Армения, Армения!

7

Не развалины — нет! — но порубка могучего циркульного леса,
Якорные пни поваленных дубов звериного и басенного
                                                христианства,
Рулоны каменного сукна на капителях — как товар
                        из языческой разграбленной лавки,
Виноградины с голубиное яйцо, завитки бараньих рогов
И нахохленные орлы с совиными крыльями, ещё
                        не осквернённые Византией.

6

A country of roaring stones—
        Armenia, Armenia!
Calling hoarse mountains to arms—
        Armenia, Armenia!

Ever flying to the silver trumpets of Asia—
        Armenia, Armenia!
Generously giving away Persian coins of the sun—
        Armenia, Armenia!

7

Not ruins—no, but a cutting-down of a mighty circular wood,
Anchor-like stubs of cut oak-trees of a wild and legendary
                                 Christendom,
Rolls of stony cloth on the capitals—like goods
                    from a plundered pagan curiosity shop,
Grapes of the size of a pigeon-egg, curls of rams' horns,
Sullen eagles with owl's wings—
                not desecrated by Byzantium yet.

8

Холодно розе в снегу:
    на Севане снег в три аршина . . .
    Вытащил горный рыбак расписные лазурные сани,
    Сытых форелей усатые морды
    несут полицейскую службу
    на известковом дне.

А в Эривани и в Эчмиадзине
    весь воздух выпила огромная гора,
    Её бы приманить какой-то окариной
    Иль дудкой приручить, чтоб таял снег во рту.

Снега, снега, снега на рисовой бумаге,
    Гора плывет к губам.
    Мне холодно. Я рад . . .

9

Какая роскошь в нищенском селеньи —
Волосяная музыка воды!
Что это? Пряжа? Звук? Предупрежденье?
Чур-чур меня! Далёко ль до беды!

И в лабиринте влажного распева
Такая душная стрекочет мгла,
Как будто в гости водяная дева
К часовщику подземному пришла.

8

A rose is cold in the snow,
    seven feet of snow on lake Sevan . . .
    A highlander-fisherman pulled out painted azure sledges,
    fat-whiskered faces of trouts
    are on police patrol
    on the limestone bottom.

Yet, in Yerevan and in Echmiadzin
    a giant mountain has drunk all the air,
    If it could be charmed by some ocarina
    Or tamed by a pipe, so the snow would melt in its mouth.

Snow, snow, snow on rice paper,
    The mountain flows closer to lips,
    I'm cold. I'm happy. I'm glad . . .

9

    It's such a luxury in a poor village
    To hear water's hirsute music!
    What is it? Spinning? A sound? A warning?
    Keep off! Don't trouble trouble!

    And in the moist song's maze
    There's a clatter of such a damp haze,
    As if a mermaid came to visit
    An underworld watchmaker there.

10

О порфирные цокая граниты,
Спотыкается крестьянская лошадка,
Забираясь на лысый цоколь
Государственного звонкого камня.
А за нею с узелками сыра,
Еле дух переводя, бегут курдины,
Примирившие дьявола и Бога,
Каждому воздавши половину.

24 октября 1930, Тифлис

11

Лазурь да глина, глина да лазурь.
Чего ж тебе ещё? Скорей глаза сощурь,
Как близорукий шах над перстнем бирюзовым, —
Над книгой звонких глин, над книжною землёй,
Над гнойной книгою, над глиной дорогой,
Которой мучимся, как музыкой и словом.

12

Я тебя никогда не увижу,
Близорукое армянское небо,
И уже не взгляну, прищурясь,
На дорожный шатёр Арарата,
И уже никогда не раскрою
В библиотеке авторов гончарных
Прекрасной земли пустотелую книгу,
По которой учились первые люди.

16 октября–5 ноября 1930, Тифлис

10

Clanking on regal granites,
The peasant's horse stumbles,
Climbing a bald socle
Of the state's resonant stone.
Behind her, carrying sacks with cheese,
Barely catching their breath, run the Kurds,
Who reconciled Satan with God,
Giving a half to each.

October 24, 1930, Tiflis

11

Azure and clay, clay and azure skies,
What else do you want? Squint your eyes,
As a short-sighted shah over a turquoise ring,
Over the book of ringing clay, a bookish land,
Over a festering book, dear clay,
Which tortures us like music and the word.

12

I will never see you again,
A nearsighted Armenian sky,
Looking at Mount Ararat's tent,
I will never squint my eye,
Nor will I ever open again
A hollow book of a wonderful land
In the library of pottery authors,
From which the first people learned.

October16–November 5, 1930, Tiflis

* * *

На полицейской бумаге верже
Ночь наглоталась колючих ершей.
Звёзды живут — канцелярские птички,
Пишут и пишут свои раппортички.

Сколько бы им ни хотелось мигать,
Могут они заявленье подать —
И на мерцанье, писанье и тленье
Возобновляют всегда разрешенье.

октябрь 1930, Тифлис

* * *

On the police laid paper the night
Swallowed a mouthful of prickly pikes.
The stars live like office birds,
They keep writing their rep-ports.*

Wherever they'd like to resort to twinkling,
They should write to the higher commission—
And for twinkling, writing, and dwindling
They will always issue permission.

October 1930, Tiflis

---

*   The original is spelled *rapportichki*, alluding to the leftist pro-Soviet writers' union, Russian Association of Proletarian Writers [Rossiiskaia assotsiatsiia proletarskikh pisatelei, abbriviated as RAPP].

* * *

Не говори никому,
Всё, что ты видел, забудь —
Птицу, старуху, тюрьму
Или ещё что-нибудь ...

Или охватит тебя,
Только уста разомкнёшь,
При наступлении дня
Мелкая хвойная дрожь.

Вспомнишь на даче осу,
Детский чернильный пенал
Или чернику в лесу,
Что никогда не сбирал.

октябрь 1930, Тифлис

* * *

Don't tell it anyone—forget
Everything you have seen—
A prison, an old woman, a bird
Or whatever it could have been . . .

Lest, should you open your mouth
At dawn or in broad daylight,
You'll be shaken at once
By a rapid coniferous trance.

You'll remember a rural wasp,
A student's pencil-case
Or forest blueberries—those
You never picked up.

October 1930, Tiflis

* * *

Колючая речь Араратской долины,
Дикая кошка — армянская речь,
Хищный язык городов глинобитных,
Речь голодающих кирпичей.

А близорукое шахское небо —
Слепорождённая бирюза —
Всё не прочтёт пустотелую книгу
Чёрною кровью запёкшихся глин.

октябрь 1930, Тифлис

* * *

A prickly speech of the Ararat Valley,
A wild cat, the Armenian tongue,
A wild tongue of clay-built towns,
The speech of starving stones.

While a shortsighted shah's sky—
Azure born blind—
Fails to read a hollow book
With the black clotted blood of clay.

October 1930, Tiflis

* * *

Как люб мне натугой живущий,
Столетьем считающий год,
Рожающий, спящий, орущий,
К земле пригвождённый народ.

Твоё пограничное ухо —
Все звуки ему хороши,
Желтуха, желтуха, желтуха
В проклятой горчичной глуши!

октябрь 1930, Тифлис

* * *

How dear to me are those people
Counting ages like years,
Giving birth, sleeping, and yelling,
With their strained lives pinned to earth.

You have a frontier ear—
All the sounds seem pleasant to it,
It's jaundice, a yellow fever, it's yellow—
In damned mustard boondocks they strife!

October 1930, Tiflis

* * *

Дикая кошка — армянская речь
Мучит меня и царапает ухо.
Хоть на постели горбатой прилечь —
О, лихорадка, о, злая моруха!

Падают вниз с потолка светляки,
Ползают мухи по липкой простыне,
И маршируют повзводно полки
Птиц голенастых по жёлтой равнине.

Страшен чиновник — лицо как тюфяк,
Нету его ни жалчей, ни нелепей,
Командированный — мать твою так! —
Без подорожной в армянские степи.

Пропадом ты пропади, говорят,
Сгинь ты навек, чтоб ни слуху, ни духу, —
Старый повытчик, награбив деньжат,
Бывший гвардеец, замыв оплеуху.

Грянет ли в двери знакомое: — «Ба!
Ты ли, дружище?» Какая издёвка!
Долго ль ещё нам ходить по гроба,
Как по грибы деревенская девка? . .

Были мы люди, а стали людьё,
И суждено — по какому разряду? —
Нам роковое в груди колотьё
Да эрзерумская кисть винограду.

ноябрь 1930, Тифлис

* * *

A wild cat—the Armenian speech
Tortures me and scratches my ear.
I'd rather lie down on a humpback couch—
Oh, evil dark spell, oh, fever.

Fireflies fall down from the ceiling,
Flies crawl on a clammy linen,
And the armies of long-legged birds
March platoon by platoon on a yellow plain.

A fearful bureaucrat with his mattress-like face,
No one is more absurd and wretched than he,
Sent on assignment—goddamn fate—
Without papers to Armenian steppes.

Devil take you, vanish, they say,
So that there is no sight, no sound of you—
An old official who stole cash,
A former guardsman who took a slap in the face.

Will a familiar—"Wow! Is that you, old chap?"—
Greet you in the doorway—such a disgrace!
How long will we be gathering coffins
Like a country girl goes picking mushrooms? . . .

We were people and now we are scum,
Doomed to the fateful—what class?—
Heart rapture and gripes
And—Erzurumian cluster of grapes.

November 1930, Tiflis

* * *

Ma voix aigre et fausse…

Verlain

Я скажу тебе с последней
     Прямотой:
Всё лишь бредни, шерри-бренди,
     Ангел мой.

Там, где эллину сияла
     Красота,
Мне из чёрных дыр зияла
     Срамота.

Греки сбондили Елену
     По волнам,
Ну а мне — солёной пеной
     По губам.

По губам меня помажет
     Пустота,
Строгий кукиш мне покажет
     Нищета.

Ой ли, так ли, дуй ли, вей ли,
     Всё равно.
Ангел Мэри, пей коктейли,
     Дуй вино!

Я скажу тебе с последней
     Прямотой:
Всё лишь бредни, шерри-бренди,
     Ангел мой.

Москва, март 1931

* * *

Ma voix aigre et fausse . . .*

Verlain

I will tell you this, my lady,
    With final candor,
All is folly, sherry-brandy,
    Oh, my angel.

Where Beauty shone
    To a Hellene,
Disgrace gaped at me
    From a black hole.

Greeks stole Helen
    Along the sea,
While I taste a salty brine
    On my lips.

Void will soil my lips
    And disgrace,
Poverty will cock a grim snook
    At my face.

Oh, lo, is that so, drink or sail,
    It's all the same.
Angel Mary, drink your cocktail,
    Gulp your wine!

I will tell you this, my lady,
    With final candor,
All is folly, sherry-brandy,
    Oh, my angel.

Moscow, March 1931

---

*   "My shrill and false voice," from Paul Verlain's "Sérénade" (published in his 1866 collection).

* * *

За гремучую доблесть грядущих веков,
За высокое племя людей —
Я лишился и чаши на пире отцов,
И веселья, и чести своей.

Мне на плечи кидается век-волкодав,
Но не волк я по крови своей —
Запихай меня лучше, как шапку в рукав
Жаркой шубы сибирских степей,

Чтоб не видеть ни труса, ни хлипкой грязцы,
Ни кровавых костей в колесе,
Чтоб сияли всю ночь голубые песцы
Мне в своей первобытной красе, —

Уведи меня в ночь, где течёт Енисей
И сосна до звезды достаёт,
Потому что не волк я по крови своей
И меня только равный убьёт.

17–28 марта 1931

* * *

For the thunderous courage of ages to come,
For the lofty race of men—
I'm deprived of the cup at my forefathers' feast,
Of my honor, my joy, and my mirth.

The wolfhound-age flings itself at my back,
But I am not a wolf by my blood—
You'd better stuff me like a hat in the sleeve
Of the hot fur-coat of the Siberian wood,

So that I see no coward, no vile weak flesh,
Nor the bloody bones in the wheel,
But the blue foxes may shine all night long
In their primal beauty to me—

Take me away into the night to the Yenisei
Where the star is touched by a pine-tree,
For I am not a wolf by my blood,
And only my equal can kill me.

March 17–28, 1931

* * *

Нет, не спрятаться мне от великой муры
За извозчичью спину Москвы.
Я — трамвайная вишенка страшной поры
И не знаю, зачем я живу.

Мы с тобою поедем на «А» и на «Б»
Посмотреть, кто скорее умрёт,
А она то сжимается, как воробей,
То растёт, как воздушный пирог.

И едва успевает грозить из угла —
«Ты как хочешь, а я не рискну!» —
У кого под перчаткой не хватит тепла,
Чтоб объехать всю курву-Москву.

апрель 1931

* * *

No, I won't be able to hide from a great mess
Behind Moscow's broad coachman's back.
I am a streetcar cherry of the terrible days,
And I don't know what I live for.

We'll take street cars "A" and "B"
To see who will die first,
While Moscow ruffles up like a sparrow
Or rises like a pie on the yeast of air.

It nearly manages to ambush us everywhere—
"You may try, but I will not dare!"
Whoever has warmth under one's underwear
To run around all Moscow, this whore!

April 1931

Неправда

Я с дымящей лучиной вхожу
К шестипалой неправде в избу:
— Дай-ка я на тебя погляжу —
Ведь лежать мне в сосновом гробу.

А она мне солёных грибков
Вынимает в горшке из-под нар,
А она из ребячьих пупков
Подаёт мне горячий отвар.

— Захочу, — говорит, — дам ещё …
Ну, а я не дышу, сам не рад …
Шасть к порогу — куда там … В плечо
Уцепилась и тащит назад.

Вошь да глушь у неё, тишь да мша,
Полуспаленка, полутюрьма.
— Ничего, хороша, хороша …
Я и сам ведь такой же, кума.

4 апреля 1931, Москва

Untruth

I come with a smoking torch
In the hut of a six-fingered untruth:
—Let me look at you, let me watch,
Since I'll be laid in a pine coffin, struth.

She treats me with pickled mushrooms,
Takes a pot from under her plank-bed
And serves a fresh nourishing broth
Cooked from the babies' navels.

—"If I want, I'll pour you some more . . ."
I am so scared I can barely breathe . . .
I tried to run to the door—oh, no go . . .
She grabbed my shoulder and dragged me back.

Peace and moss in her hut, nice and lice,
In the back of beyond bedroom-cell.
—You are good, you are good, all is nice . . .
We are birds of one feather—in hell.

April 4, 1931

* * *

Полночь в Москве. Роскошно буддийское лето.
С дроботом мелким расходятся улицы в чоботах узких, железных,
В чёрной оспе блаженствуют кольца бульваров.
    Нет на Москву и ночью угомону,
    Когда покой бежит из-под копыт . . .
    Ты скажешь: где-то там на полигоне
    Два клоуна засели — Бим и Бом,
    И в ход пошли гребенки, молоточки,
    То слышится гармоника губная,
    То детское молочное пьянино:
    До-ре-ми-фа
    И соль-фа-ми-ре-до.

Бывало, я, как помоложе, выйду
В проклеенном резиновом пальто
В широкую разлапицу бульваров,
Где спичечные ножки цыганочки в подоле бьются длинном,
Где арестованный медведь гуляет —
Самой природы вечный меньшевик.
    И пахло до отказу лавровишней! . .
    Куда же ты? Ни лавров нет, ни вишен . . .

Я подтяну бутылочную гирьку
Кухонных крупно скачущих часов.
Уж до чего шероховато время,
А всё-таки люблю за хвост его ловить:
Ведь в беге собственном оно не виновато
Да, кажется, чуть-чуть жуликовато.

* * *

Midnight in Moscow. A Buddhist summer is lavish.
With a rapid tapping the streets pass by in their narrow iron boots.
The rings of the boulevards delight in chicken pox.*
      Even at night Moscow is restless,
      When rest runs away under the hooves . . .
      You'll say: somewhere at the firing ground
      Two clowns entrenched themselves—Bim and Bom,
      And they put to use hammers, combs,
      One hears either a mouth harmonica
      Or a milk-fed baby piano:
      Do-re-mi-fa
      And sol-fa-mi-re-do.

When I was younger, I used to go out
In a taped rubber coat
Into wide-branched boulevards
Where a gypsy woman's feet, thin as matches, beat under a long skirt,
And an arrested bear walks,
An eternal Menshevik of Nature.
      And the smell of cherry-laurels used to fill you up choke-full.
      Where to go? There are neither cherries nor laurels . . .

I will pull up a bottle-like weight
Of a wildly racing kitchen clock.
Time is too rough,
But I like to catch it by its tail:
Since it can't be blamed for its rush,
Yet it still seems a bit of a swindler.

*   A visual image alluding to the bloom of poplar trees that at the time of Mandelstam were planted along the Boulevard Ring of Moscow. After the poplar seeds are dispersed in the air, empty black or brown boxes fall down to the ground. In Billie Holiday's song "Strange Fruit," there is a line: "Black bodies swinging in the southern breeze / Strange fruit hanging from the poplar trees. . . ."

Чур! Не просить, не жаловаться, цыц!
Не хныкать!
        Для того ли разночинцы
Рассохлые топтали сапоги, чтоб я теперь их предал?
          Мы умрём как пехотинцы,
          Но не прославим ни хищи, ни поденщины, ни лжи.

Есть у нас паутинка шотландского старого пледа,
Ты меня им укроешь, как флагом военным, когда я умру.
Выпьем, дружок, за наше ячменное горе,
        Выпьем до дна!

Из густо отработавших кино,
Убитые, как после хлороформа,
Выходят толпы. До чего они венозны,
И до чего им нужен кислород!

Пора вам знать: я тоже современник,
Я человек эпохи Москвошвея,
Смотрите, как на мне топорщится пиджак,
Как я ступать и говорить умею!
        Попробуйте меня от века оторвать,
         Ручаюсь вам — себе свернёте шею!

Я говорю с эпохою, но разве
Душа у ней пеньковая и разве
Она у нас постыдно прижилась,
Как сморщенный зверёк в тибетском храме:
Почешется — и в цинковую ванну, —
Изобрази ещё нам, Марь Иванна!
        Пусть это оскорбительно — поймите:
        Есть блуд труда и он у нас в крови.

Let's not hang head, don't complain! Shut up!
Stop whining!
      Did *raznochintsy**
Wear out their cracked boots, for me to betray them now?
      We'll die like infantry
      But won't hail day labor, theft and lies.

We have a cobweb of an old Scottish plaid,
You'll cover me with it when I die.
Let's drink, my dear, to our barley grief,
      Bottoms up!

From heavily labored cinemas
As if killed by chloroform
Crowds walk out—so varicose they are,
They need oxygen so bad!

It's time you knew: I'm a contemporary too,
I am a man of Moscow's ready-made apparel's epoch,
Look, how my jacket bulges,
How I can step and walk!
      Try to tear me off the age,
      I guarantee—you'll break you neck!

I am speaking with the epoch, but does
She have a hempen soul, and has
She shamefully settled down in our place
Like a shrunk small beast in a Tibet temple:
She would scratch her back—and plunge into a zinc bath.
—Mary Doe, show us some more!
      Perhaps it is insulting—but you get to realize:
      There is a lust of labor and it's in our blood.

---

*   Originally, "people of miscellaneous ranks," later used to denote persons of non-noble origin who due to their education were excluded from taxable status and could apply for personal distinguished citizenship. In the nineteenth century, the term was associated with democratic, liberal-minded intellectuals (intelligentsia) who sacrificed their lives for the common good, educating and enlightening Russian peasants and workers. See also note 89 on p. 48.

Уже светает. Шумят сады зелёным телеграфом.
К Рембрандту входит в гости Рафаэль.
Он с Моцартом в Москве души не чает —
За карий глаз, за воробьиный хмель.
И, словно пневматическую почту
Иль студенец медузы черноморской,
Передают с квартиры на квартиру
Конвейером воздушным сквозняки,
Как майские студенты-шелапуты...

май — 4 июня 1931

The day is breaking. The gardens rustle like a green telegraph.
And Rembrandt is visited by Rafael.
Rafael thinks the world of Mozart in Moscow—
For his brown eyes and a sparrow booze.
And like pneumatic mail
Or the gelatin of a Black Sea jellyfish,
Like an air conveyer, draughts
Are transmitted from one flat to another,
Like pranksters-students do in May . . .

May–June 4, 1931

Отрывки из уничтоженных стихов

1

В год тридцать первый от рожденья века
Я возвратился, нет — читай: насильно
Был возвращён в буддийскую Москву.
А перед тем я всё-таки увидел
Библейской скатертью богатый Арарат
И двести дней провел в стране субботней,
Которую Арменией зовут.

Захочешь пить — там есть вода такая
Из курдского источника Арзни,
Хорошая, колючая, сухая
И самая правдивая вода.

2

Уж я люблю московские законы,
Уж не скучаю по воде Арзни.
В Москве черёмухи да телефоны,
И казнями там имениты дни.

Excerpts from Destroyed Poems

1

On the thirty-first year from this century's birth
I came back, no, read: was forced
To return to the Buddhist Moscow.
Yet, I was able to see before that
Rich Ararat's Biblical table cloth
And spent two hundred days in the Sabbath land,
Which is called Armenia.

If you are thirsty—there is water there
From the Kurdish spring Arzni,
Good, prickly, dry,
And most truthful water.

2

I have already loved Moscow laws
And stopped missing the water of Arzni.
There are bird cherry trees and telephones
And executions there distinguish our days.

3

Захочешь жить, тогда глядишь с улыбкой
На молоко с буддийской синевой,
Проводишь взглядом барабан турецкий,
Когда обратно он на красных дрогах
Несётся вскачь с гражданских похорон,
Иль встретишь воз с поклажей из подушек
И скажешь: гуси-лебеди, домой!

Не разбирайся, щёлкай, милый кодак,
Покуда глаз — хрусталик кравчей птицы,
А не стекляшка!
    Больше светотени —
Ещё, ещё! Сетчатка голодна!

4

Я больше не ребёнок!
              Ты, могила,
Не смей учить горбатого — молчи!
Я говорю за всех с такою силой,
Чтоб нёбо стало небом, чтобы губы
Потрескались, как розовая глина.

6 июня 1931, Москва

3

If you are thirsty, then look with a smile
At the milk with a Buddhist blue hue,
Following a Turkish drum with your eye,
When it rushes in the red hearse
From civil funerals back,
Or you meet a wagon carrying a load of pillows
And say: go, geese and swans, home!

Don't be too fussy, click, sweet Kodak,
While an eye is a pupil of a royal carver's bird,
Not just a piece of glass!
    More light and shade
More, chiaroscuro,—my retina is starving!

4

I am no longer a child!
                You, grave,
Don't dare teach a humpback—shut your mouth!*
I speak for everyone with such a force
That my palate turned into a sky dome
So that my lips crack like pink clay.

June 6, 1931, Moscow

---

* An allusion to the Russian proverb "the grave will fix the humpback"—that is, a leopard cannot change its spots.

* * *

Ещё далёко мне до патриарха,
Ещё на мне полупочтенный возраст,
Ещё меня ругают за глаза
На языке трамвайных перебранок,
В котором нет ни смысла, ни аза:
Такой-сякой! Ну что ж, я извиняюсь, —
Но в глубине ничуть не изменяюсь …

Когда подумаешь, чем связан с миром,
То сам себе не веришь: ерунда!
Полночный ключик от чужой квартиры,
Да гривенник серебряный в кармане,
Да целлулоид фильмы воровской.

Я, как щенок, бросаюсь к телефону
На каждый истерический звонок.
В нём слышно польское: «Дзенкую, пане!»,
Иногородний ласковый упрёк
Иль неисполненное обещанье.

Всё думаешь, к чему бы приохотиться
Посереди хлопушек и шутих;
Перекипишь — а там, гляди, останется
Одна сумятица да безработица —
Пожалуйста, прикуривай у них!

То усмехнусь, то робко приосанюсь
И с белорукой тростью выхожу:
Я слушаю сонаты в переулках,
У всех лотков облизываю губы,
Листаю книги в глыбких подворотнях,
И не живу, но всё-таки живу.

* * *

I am far from being as old as patriarch,
I am still of half-respected age,
They still scold me behind my back
In the vernacular of a street-car squabble,
Which doesn't have a grain of sense:
You so-and-so! Well, I excuse myself,—
But in the depth of my soul don't change a bit.

When one would think what binds you to this world,
You won't believe yourself: it's such a smidge!
A midnight key to someone else's dwelling,
A silver dime in the pocket, and
A celluloid of a movie about thieves.

Like a puppy, I rush to the telephone,
Answering each hysterical call.
I hear "Dziękuję, panu!"* in Polish,
A foreign tender reproach
Or an unfulfilled promise.

You think what should you stick to
Amidst flip–flaps and flappers;
You will burn out—and then look, what's left:
Just some turmoil and unemployment—
So, if you like, light your cigarette from them!

I chuckle or thrust out my chest shyly
And go out with a blonde walking cane:
I listen to sonatas in the lane,
I lick my lips at every booth,
I list through books in deep backstreets,
And I don't live but I do live.

---

*   Thank you, sir (Polish).

Я к воробьям пойду и к репортёрам,
Я к уличным фотографам пойду,
И в пять минут — лопаткой из ведёрка —
Я получу своё изображенье
Под конусом лиловой шах-горы.

А иногда пущусь на побегушки
В распаренные душные подвалы,
Где чистые и честные китайцы
Хватают палочками шарики из теста,
Играют в узкие нарезанные карты
И водку пьют, как ласточки с Янцзы.

Люблю разъезды скворчущих трамваев,
И астраханскую икру асфальта,
Накрытого соломенной рогожей,
Напоминающей корзинку асти,
И страусовы перья арматуры
В начале стройки ленинских домов.

Вхожу в вертепы чудные музеев,
Где пучатся кащеевы Рембрандты,
Достигнув блеска кордованской кожи;
Дивлюсь рогатым митрам Тициана,
И Тинторетто пёстрому дивлюсь —
За тысячу крикливых попугаев.

И до чего хочу я разыграться,
Разговориться — выговорить правду —
Послать хандру к туману, к бесу, к ляду, —
Взять за руку кого-нибудь: будь ласков, —
Сказать ему, — нам по пути с тобой…

Москва, июль — сентябрь 1931

I'll go to the reporters and to sparrows
And to the street photographers I'll go:
Five minutes—and with a little spade
From a small pail—I'll get my image
Under a cone of a violet Shakh-mount.*

And sometimes I would run on errands
Into the steamy stuffy basements,
Where clean and honest Chinese
Grab dough balls with their sticks,
Play narrow hand-made cards and
Drink vodka like swallows from the Yangtze.

I like how sizzling street cars ride,
I like the black caviar of asphalt
Covered with straw matting
Resembling a basket of Asti,
And ostrich feathers of rebars
In the beginning of Lenin's house constructions.

I go into the miraculous caves of museums
Where Kashchey's Rembrandts stare,
Reaching the luster of Cordovan leather;
I wonder at Titian's horned forked caps
And I am amazed by pied Tintoretto—
Like a thousand clamorous parrots.

I want so much to play around:
To talk—to tell the whole truth out loud—
To tell my spleen to go to blues, to hell,
Take someone by the hand: be kind,**—
Tell him: I'm going the same way as you . . .

July–September, 1931, Moscow

---

*   In Turkic languages Shakhtau Mount, otherwise known as Elbrus.

**   "Be kind" is the literal translation of the Ukrainian phrase for "please" (*bud' laska*).

* * *

Сегодня можно снять декалькомани,
Мизинец окунув в Москву-реку,
С разбойника-Кремля. Какая прелесть
Фисташковые эти голубятни:
Хоть проса им насыпать, хоть овса…
А в недорослях кто? Иван Великий —
Великовозрастная колокольня.
Стоит себе ещё болван болваном
Который век. Его бы за границу,
Чтоб доучился… Да куда там! стыдно!

Река Москва в четырёхтрубном дыме
И перед нами весь раскрытый город —
Купальщики-заводы и сады
Замоскворецкие. Не так ли,
Откинув палисандровую крышку
Огромного концертного рояля,
Мы проникаем в звучное нутро?
        Белогвардейцы, вы его видали?
        Рояль Москвы слыхали? Гули-гули!..

Мне кажется, как всякое другое,
Ты, время, незаконно! Как мальчишка
За взрослыми в морщинистую воду,
Я, кажется, в грядущее вхожу,
И, кажется, его я не увижу…

Уж я не выйду в ногу с молодёжью
На разлинованные стадионы,
Разбуженный повесткой мотоцикла,
Я на рассвете не вскочу с постели,
В стеклянные дворцы на курьих ножках
Я даже тенью лёгкой не войду…

* * *

Today we can take decals
Of the bandit-Kremlin, having dipped
A little finger in the Moskva-river. How sweet
Are these pistachio-colored dovecotes:
You can feed them with some millet or oats . . .
And who is a young oaf? Ivan the Great—
An overgrown bell tower.
It stands like stupid is like stupid does
For centuries. It should be sent abroad
To finish education . . . Yet, too shameful!

The Moskva–river is wrapped in a four-chimney's smoke,*
And the city is opened to us all:
Swimmers-plants and gardens
Behind the Moskva-river district. Don't we
Enter the inner resonance, having opened
The enormous grand piano's palisander cover?
White Guards, have you seen it?
        Have you heard the Moskva-river piano?
        Cock-a-doodle-do! Adieu! . .

It seems to me, you, time, are as illegitimate
As any other! Following adults,
I plunge into a wrinkly water like a boy,
I seem to enter the approaching future,
And it looks like I won't see it . . .

I won't go into the ruled stadiums
Following the young, and woken up
By the summons of a motorbike,
I won't jump out of bed at dawn,
I won't be able to enter even as a shadow
The glassy palaces on chicken legs . . .

---

*   "Four-chimney smoke" refers to the coal burning power plant with smoke stacks, Moscow, Russia: https://www.123rf.com/photo_33181055_coal-burning-power-plant-with-smoke-stacks-moscow-russia.html

Мне с каждым днём дышать всё тяжелее,
А между тем нельзя повременить . . .
И рождены для наслажденья бегом
Лишь сердце человека и коня.

И Фауста бес, сухой и моложавый,
Вновь старику кидается в ребро
И подбивает взять почасно ялик,
Или махнуть на Воробьёвы горы,
Иль на трамвае охлестнуть Москву.

Ей некогда — она сегодня в няньках,
Всё мечется — на сорок тысяч люлек
Она одна — и пряжа на руках…

Какое лето! Молодых рабочих
Татарские сверкающие спины
С девической повязкой на хребтах,
Таинственные узкие лопатки
И детские ключицы…
                    Здравствуй, здравствуй,
Могучий некрещёный позвоночник,
С которым проживём не век, не два!..

25 июня 1931, Москва

It's getting hard to breathe in every day,
But I can't make a pause nor have some rest . . .
Only the hearts of man and horse
Are born for the rupture of the race.

And Faust's devil, gaunt and young, seduces me,
Gray hair, nourished with green thoughts,
Enticing me to rent a rowing boat
Or just to go to Sparrow Hills,
Or circle Moscow in a street car.

She is pressed for time—she is a nanny
Rushing amidst four thousand cradles
Alone and also has to spin her yarn . . .

What a summer! Young workers'
Shining Tartar spines
With a maiden's strip on their backbones,
Mysteriously narrow shoulder blades
And children's collar bones . . .
                    Hello, hello,
A mighty unchristened backbone
With which we'll live for more than age or two! . .

June 25, 1931, Moscow

Ламарк

Был старик, застенчивый как мальчик,
Неуклюжий, робкий патриарх . . .
Кто за честь природы фехтовальщик?
Ну, конечно, пламенный Ламарк.

Если всё живое лишь помарка
За короткий выморочный день,
На подвижной лестнице Ламарка
Я займу последнюю ступень.

К кольчецам спущусь и к усоногим,
Прошуршав средь ящериц и змей,
По упругим сходням, по излогам
Сокращусь, исчезну, как Протей.

Роговую мантию надену,
От горячей крови откажусь,
Обрасту присосками и в пену
Океана завитком вопьюсь.

Мы прошли разряды насекомых
С наливными рюмочками глаз.
Он сказал: природа вся в разломах,
Зренья нет — ты зришь в последний раз.

Он сказал: довольно полнозвучья,
Ты напрасно Моцарта любил,
Наступает глухота паучья,
Здесь провал сильнее наших сил.

И от нас природа отступила
Так, как будто мы ей не нужны,
И продольный мозг она вложила,
Словно шпагу, в тёмные ножны.

Lamarck

He was an old man, shy as a boy,
An awkward timid patriarch . . .
Who fenced to defend nature's honor?
It was certainly fiery Lamarck.

If all living nature is but an error
Of a short nightmarish day,
I will take the lowest stair
On Lamark's flexible scale.

I'll go down to barnacles and worms,
Sizzle among lizards and snakes,
Down the hollows, down the lithe pathways,
I'll contract and, like Proteus, wane.

I'll put a corneous mantle on,
Abandon hot blood and grow
Suckers, sink into an ocean's foam
As a tendril of some anemone.

We have passed the class of insects
With full goblets of eyes.
He says that nature abounds in fractures,
There's no vision—you see for the last time.

He says: the resonance will cease,
You loved Mozart in vain:
A spider's deafness will seize
You—this gap is beyond our gain.

Nature has turned away
As if she didn't need us anymore,
And she put our medulla, spine cord,
In a dark sheathe like a sword.

И подъёмный мост она забыла,
Опоздала опустить для тех,
У кого зелёная могила,
Красное дыханье, гибкий смех...

7–9 мая 1932

She was late or just forgot
To put down a drawbridge for those
Who have a green grave,
A lithe laughter, a red breath . . .

May 7–9, 1932

Импрессионизм

Художник нам изобразил
Глубокий обморок сирени
И красок звучные ступени
На холст, как струпья, положил.

Он понял масла густоту:
Его запёкшееся лето
Лиловым мозгом разогрето,
Расширенное в духоту.

А тень-то, тень — всё лиловéй!
Свисток иль хлыст как спичка тухнет.
Ты скажешь: повара на кухне
Готовят жирных голубей.

Угадывается качель,
Недомалёваны вуали,
И в этом сумрачном развале
Уже хозяйничает шмель.

Москва, 23 мая 1932

Impressionism

The artist painted
How deeply lilacs fainted,
Ply over ply, resounding colors
He dabbed like scabs on canvas.

He realized the thickness of oil:
He made his clotted summer boil
Heated by a violent violet mind
Expanded in a sultry daylight.

A shade grows more violet with each touch!
A whistle or a whip dies like a match.
You'll say: chefs in the kitchens
Are cooking now fat pigeons.

There is a hint of a swing,
Veils are vague, I guess,
And a bumblebee, a king,
Reigns in this summer mess.

Moscow, May 23, 1932

Батюшков

Словно гуляка с волшебною тростью,
Батюшков нежный со мною живёт.
Он тополями шагает в замостье,
Нюхает розу и Дафну поёт.

Ни на минуту не веря в разлуку,
Кажется, я поклонился ему —
В светлой перчатке холодную руку
Я с лихорадочной завистью жму.

Он усмехнулся. Я молвил: спасибо.
И не нашёл от смущения слов:
Ни у кого — этих звуков изгибы,
И никогда — этот говор валов…

Наше мученье и наше богатство,
Косноязычный, с собой он принёс
Шум стихотворства и колокол братства
И гармонический проливень слёз.

И отвечал мне оплакавший Тасса:
Я к величаньям ещё не привык,
Только стихов виноградное мясо
Мне освежило случайно язык…

Что ж! Поднимай удивлённые брови
Ты, горожанин и друг горожан,
Вечные сны, как образчики крови,
Переливай из стакана в стакан…

18 июня 1932

Batiushkov

Like an idler with a magic wand,
Gentle Batiushkov lives with me.
Along the poplar alley he walks to bridgefields,
He sings Daphna and smells a rose.

Not believing in parting forever,
I bowed to him suavely,
Shaking his hand in a light glove
With a feverish envy.

He smiled, and I uttered, "Thank you,"
Being too shy to find a word:
No one has curves of such sounds,
No one else made rolling waves talk.

Our tormenter and our wealth,
Muttering and tongue-tied, he gave us
The bell of brotherhood, the noise of verse,
And a harmonious shower of tears.

The one who mourned Tasso replies:
I haven't gotten used to praise,
Only a grape flesh of verse
Refreshed my tongue sometimes.

Well, raise your brows in surprise,
You, a city dweller, a townsmen's friend,
Eternal dreams from glass to glass.
Pour like exquisite samples of blood . . .

June 18, 1932

* * *

Дайте Тютчеву стрекóзу —
Догадайтесь, почему.
Веневитинову — розу.
Ну а перстень — никому.

Баратынского подошвы
Изумили прах веков.
У него без всякой прошвы
Наволочки облаков.

А ещё над нами волен
Лермонтов — мучитель наш,
И всегда одышкой болен
Фета жирный карандаш.

А ещё, богохранима
На гвоздях торчит всегда
У ворот Ерусалима
Хомякова борода.

8 июля 1932

* * *

Give Tiutchev a dragonfly—
Guess yourselves why—
Give Venevitinov a rose,
But a signet ring to none of those.

Baratynsky's shoe soles
Amazed the centuries' dust:
Without any stitches are
His pillow cases of clouds.

Lermontov, our torturer,
Rules over us as well,
And a fat pencil of Fet
Is always short of breath.

And protected by the Lord,
Khomyakov's long beard*
Is always hanging weird
Nailed to Jerusalem's gates.

July 8, 1932

---

* Aleksey Stepanovich Khomyakov (1804–1860) was a Russian religious philosopher, theologian, and a poet. He was one of the founders of the Slavofile movement and denied both capitalism and socialism as Western influences. For Khomyakov, freedom must be actualized in *sobornost'* (religious community), not in individualism. He also saw Moscow as "the third Rome" and the center of religious life. Hence Osip Mandelstam ironically compares Moscow to Jerusalem.

Ариост

В Европе холодно. В Италии темно.
Власть отвратительна, как руки брадобрея.
О, если б распахнуть, да как нельзя скорее,
На Адриатику широкое окно.

Над розой мускусной жужжание пчелы,
В степи полуденной — кузнечик мускулистый,
Крылатой лошади подковы тяжелы,
Часы песочные желты и золотисты.

На языке цикад пленительная смесь
Из грусти пушкинской и средиземной спеси,
Как плющ назойливый, цепляющийся весь,
Он мужественно врёт, с Орландом куролеся.

Часы песочные желты и золотисты,
В степи полуденной кузнечик мускулистый,
И прямо на луну влетает враль плечистый.

Любезный Ариост, посольская лиса,
Цветущий папоротник, парусник, столетник,
Ты слушал на луне овсянок голоса,
А при дворе у рыб учёный был советник.

О город ящериц, в котором нет души,
От ведьмы и судьи таких сынов рожала
Феррара чёрствая и на цепи держала —
И солнце рыжего ума взошло в глуши.

Мы удивляемся лавчонке мясника,
Под сеткой синих мух уснувшему дитяти,
Ягнёнку на дворе, монаху на осляти,

Солдатам герцога, юродивым слегка
От винопития, чумы и чеснока,
И свежей, как заря, удивлены утрате…

Старый Крым, май 1933; Воронеж, июль 1935

Ariosto

It's cold in Europe. It's dark in Italy.
Power is disgusting like a barber's hand.
Oh, if I could, and quickly so,—I cannot stand—
Wide open a broad window on the Adriatic Sea.

Over a musky rose—a buzzing of a bee,
A muscular grasshopper in a midday steppe, and
The horseshoes of a winged horse are heavy,
An hourglass is full of yellow and golden sand.

In the cicada's tongue, a captivating blend
Of Pushkin's sadness and Mediterranean pride,
Like clinging, clutching ivy's sprouts protend,
He played pranks with Orlando and boldly lied.

The hourglass is full of yellow and golden sand.
A muscular grasshopper in a midday steppe, and
On the moon will a broad-shouldered liar land.

A courteous Ariosto, an embassy fox, a coon,
A blooming fern, a sail, assail, astonish,
You heard the voices of thrushes on the moon
And served as a learned counselor at the court of fish.

O, city of lizards without a soul, you bore
Your sons conceived by witches from the judges,
Hard-hearted Ferrara, you kept them on a chain,
While in the wilderness the sun of reddish wisdom rose.

We are amazed by a butcher's little store,
By a baby sleeping under the net of bluish flies,
By a lamb on a hill, a monk on a donkey, by

The duke's soldiers stupefied by wine,
By garlic, plague, and then by the demise—
The loss, fresh as a dawn, shocks us as a surprise.

Old Crimea, May 1933; Voronezh, July 1935

* * *

Не искушай чужих наречий, но постарайся их забыть:
Ведь всё равно ты не сумеешь стекло зубами укусить!

О, как мучительно даётся чужого клёкота почёт:
За беззаконные восторги лихая плата стережёт!

Ведь умирающее тело и мыслящий бессмертный рот
В последний раз перед разлукой чужое имя не спасёт.

Что, если Ариост и Тассо, обворожающие нас,
Чудовища с лазурным мозгом и чешуёй из влажных глаз?

И в наказанье за гордыню, неисправимый звуколюб,
Получишь уксусную губку ты для изменнических губ.

май 1933, Старый Крым; 1935, Воронеж

* * *

Do not tempt foreign tongues—attempt forgetting them, alas,
Because your teeth will never bite the glass!

How painful is to share the flight of a foreign trill—
You'll get an evil pay for an unlawful thrill!

For foreign name on that last day won't save this
Dying flesh and these immortal thinking lips.

What if Tasso and Ariosto who are enchanting us
Are monsters with azure brains and scales of moistened eyes?

And as a punishment for pride, inveterate worshiper of sound,
You'll get a vinegar sponge for traitor's lips spellbound.

May 1933, Old Crimea, 1935, Voronezh

* * *

Квартира тиха, как бумага,
Пустая, без всяких затей,
И слышно, как булькает влага
По трубам внутри батарей.

Имущество в полном порядке,
Лягушкой застыл телефон,
Видавшие виды манатки
На улицу просятся вон.

А стены проклятые тонки,
И некуда больше бежать,
А я как дурак на гребёнке
Обязан кому-то играть.

Наглей комсомольской ячейки
И вузовской песни бойчей
Присевших на школьной скамейке
Учить щебетать палачей.

Пайковые книги читаю,
Пеньковые речи ловлю
И грозное баюшки-баю
Колхозному баю пою.

Какой-нибудь изобразитель,
Чесатель колхозного льна,
Чернила и крови смеситель,
Достоин такого рожна.

Какой-нибудь честный предатель,
Проваренный в чистках, как соль,
Жены и детей содержатель,
Такую ухлопает моль.

* * *

An apartment is quiet as paper
Blank, without any décor,
And inside the radiator
Liquid babbles and pours.

The possessions are all in order,
The telephone's stiff as a toad,
Our well-worn belongings
Are begging to be thrown.

There is nowhere else to run,
The damn walls are unfaithfully thin,
But I have to play like a clown
Idiotic tunes on a comb.

I have to teach hangmen to twit.
More insolent than a college song,
More arrogant than a komsomol gang,
They came to class to learn.

I read rationed books,
I hear ragged orations
And sing a stern lullaby
To the farmer's rations.

Some kind of a quack,
A picker of a kolkhoz flax,
A mixer of blood with ink
Deserves such a fate.

Some honest traitor,
Purged and cleansed like salt,
His spouse's and kids' supporter
Will crush such a huge moth.

И столько мучительной злости
Таит в себе каждый намёк,
Как будто вколачивал гвозди
Некрасова здесь молоток.

Давай же с тобой, как на плахе,
За семьдесят лет начинать —
Тебе, старику и неряхе,
Пора сапогами стучать.

И вместо ключа Ипокрены
Давнишнего страха струя
Ворвётся в халтурные стены
Московского злого жилья.

ноябрь 1933, Москва

Every hint here conceals
Such painful sound and fury,
As if Nekrasov's hammer
Pounded nails here.

Let's start preparing for the scaffold
Seventy years in advance,
It's time, an old slacker,
You stamped your boots at once.

Instead of Hippocrene's fountain
A familiar stream of dread
Will burst through the hackwork walls
Of Moscow's evil abode.

November 1933, Moscow

* * *

Мы живём, под собою не чуя страны,
Наши речи за десять шагов не слышны,
А где хватит на полразговорца,
Там припомнят кремлёвского горца.
Его толстые пальцы, как черви, жирны,
И слова, как пудовые гири, верны,
Тараканьи смеются глазища
И сияют его голенища.

А вокруг него сброд тонкошеих вождей,
Он играет услугами полулюдей.
Кто свистит, кто мяучит, кто хнычет,
Он один лишь бабачит и тычет.
Как подкову, дари́т за указом указ:
Кому в пах, кому в лоб, кому в бровь, кому в глаз.
Что ни казнь у него — то малина,
И широкая грудь осетина.

ноябрь 1933, Москва

* * *

We live without feeling our country's pulse,
We can't hear ourselves, no one hears us,
If a word is uttered by chance,
Kremlin highlander is remembered at once.
Like worms his thick fingers are fat,
His words like pound weights are correct,
His cockroach moustache is full of laughter,
His army boots shine, he is sought after

By a mob of thin-necked leaders, half-men,
He uses their service, manipulating them:
Some are meowing, or whistling, or whining,
He alone is poking, boking, and winning.
Like horseshoes, he grants his every decree
Poking some in the groin, in the brow, in the eye.
His executions are like cakes and ale,
His broad chest of Ossete eclipses the jail.

November 1933, Moscow

Восьмистишия

1

Люблю появление ткани,
Когда после двух или трёх,
А то — четырёх задыханий
Придёт выпрямительный вздох.

И дугами парусных гонок
Зелёные формы чертя,
Играет пространство спросонок —
Не знавшее люльки дитя.

ноябрь 1933, Москва, июль 1935, Воронеж

2

Люблю появление ткани,
Когда после двух или трёх,
А то — четырёх задыханий
Придёт выпрямительный вздох.

И так хорошо мне и тяжко,
Когда приближается миг,
И вдруг дуговая растяжка
Звучит в бормотаньях моих.

ноябрь 1933, Москва

Octaves

1

I love when the substance appears,
When gasping for two or three times,
Or four times you need, and it clears—
A straightening breath then arrives.

Then drawing green forms and spheres
By the arcs of fast racing sails,
Space, half-awake babe without peers,
Who never knew cradle, plays.

November 1933, Moscow, July 1935, Voronezh

2

I love when the substance appears,
When gasping for two or three times,
Or four times you need, and it clears—
A straightening breath then arrives.

And then it's so joyful and painful
When a moment approaches as bliss,
And a straightening arc is so gleeful
That my mutter with meaning it fills.

November 1933, Moscow

3

О, бабочка, о, мусульманка,
В разрезанном саване вся —
Жизняночка и умиранка,
Такая большая — сия!

С большими усами кусава
Ушла с головою в бурнус.
О, флагом развернутый саван,
Сложи свои крылья — боюсь!

ноябрь 1933, Москва

4

Шестого чувства крошечный придаток
Иль ящерицы теменной глазок,
Монастыри улиток и створчаток,
Мерцающих ресничек говорок.

Недостижимое, как это близко:
Ни развязать нельзя, ни посмотреть,
Как будто в руку вложена записка —
И на неё немедленно ответь …

май 1932, Москва

3

Oh, Moslem-butterfly,
All wrapped in a cut shroud,
Deathmonger and life-lover,
So big—this is you without doubt!

With biter's huge feelers-antennas,
You hide in a burnous your head,
Your shroud is unfolded like a banner,
Fold your wings for I certainly dread!

November 1933, Moscow

4

A tiny appendage of the sixth sense
Or lizard's parietal eye,
Monasteries of snails and shells,
And a hum of flickering cilia nearby.

Inaccessible—how close, but try to unfold:
One can neither see it nor unbind,
As if a note from somebody you hold,
And it should be immediately replied . . .

May 1932, Moscow

5

Преодолев затверженность природы,
Голуботвёрдый глаз проник в её закон:
В земной коре юродствуют породы,
И как руда из гру́ди рвётся стон.

И тянется глухой недоразвиток,
Как бы дорогой, согнутою в рог, —
Понять пространства внутренний избыток,
И лепестка, и купола залог.

январь–февраль 1934, Москва

6

Когда, уничтожив набросок,
Ты держишь прилежно в уме
Период без тягостных сносок,
Единый во внутренней тьме,

И он лишь на собственной тяге,
Зажмурившись, держится сам,
Он так же отнёсся к бумаге,
Как купол к пустым небесам.

ноябрь 1933, Москва

5

Overcoming the hardiness of nature,
A blue-firm eye has reached its law:
Under the Earth's crust the freaky layers fracture,
And like a moan from breast, then breaks the ore.

Underdeveloped feeler struggles to explore—
Along a horn-like pathway it would battle
To grasp the inner surplus of space, its core,
The source of a cupola and of a petal.

January 1934, Moscow

6

When having destroyed your draft,
You keep in your diligent mind
A period whole in its inner dark,
Without tiresome notes, it will find

Strength, self-propelled, to hold tight,
Without engine or else, with closed eyes,
Its relation to paper can be described
Like that of a cupola to the skies.

November 1933

7

И Шуберт на воде, и Моцарт в птичьем гаме,
И Гёте, свищущий на вьющейся тропе,
И Гамлет, мысливший пугливыми шагами,
Считали пульс толпы и верили толпе.

Быть может, прежде губ уже родился шёпот
И в бездревесности кружилися листы,
И те, кому мы посвящаем опыт,
До опыта приобрели черты.

январь 1934, Москва

8

И клёна зубчатая лапа
Купается в круглых углах,
И можно из бабочек крапа
Рисунки слагать на стенах.

Бывают мечети живые —
И я догадался сейчас:
Быть может, мы — Айя-София
С бесчисленным множеством глаз.

ноябрь 1933–январь 1934, Москва

7

Both Schubert on the water and Mozart in birds' chirping,
And Goethe whistling on a winding path,
And even Hamlet in his thoughts so fearfully stepping—
They all believed the crowd and felt its pulse.

Perhaps the whisper has been born before the lips,
And the leaves flew before the trees grew,
And those to whom we devote our experience as bliss
Acquire their form before we do.

January 1934, Moscow

8

And the jagged bough of a maple-tree
Bathes in round corners and thrives,
And one can draw pictures on the walls
With the specks of dust from butterflies.

Things like living mosques do appear,
And I suddenly now realize:
Perhaps we are all Hagia Sophia
With a countless multitude of eyes.

November 1933, Moscow

9

Скажи мне, чертёжник пустыни,
Арабских песков геометр,
Ужели безудержность линий
Сильнее, чем дующий ветр?

— Меня не касается трепет
Его иудейских забот —
Он опыт из лепета лепит
И лепет из опыта пьёт.

ноябрь 1933, Москва

10

В игольчатых чумных бокалах
Мы пьём наважденье причин,
Касаемся крючьями малых,
Как лёгкая смерть, величин.

И там, где сцепились бирюльки,
Ребёнок молчанье хранит —
Большая вселенная в люльке
У маленькой вечности спит.

ноябрь 1933, Москва

9

Tell me, a draftsman of the desert,
A geometrician of Arabian sands,
Will the lines unrestrained exert
The power of a violent wind?

—I am not concerned with the tremor,
The awe of his Judean concerns:
He molds his experience from murmur,
And his murmur he drinks from what he learns.

November 1933

10

We drink the enchantment of causes
From the flutes full of needles and plague
And hook infinitesimal numbers,
Which look like an easy light death.

And a child is stricken by silence
Where trifles would grapple and play:
A big universe peacefully slumbers
In the cradle of little eternity.

November 1933, Moscow

11

И я выхожу из пространства
В запущенный сад величин
И мнимое рву постоянство
И самосогласье причин.

И твой, бесконечность, учебник
Читаю один, без людей —
Безлиственный дикий лечебник,
Задачник огромных корней.

ноябрь 1933

11

So I leave space for a wild garden
Of values and break at my will
A seeming permanence and coherence of causes,
And there, alone and tranquil,

Infinity, I read your textbook,
Which can offer solutions and heal,
A leafless and wild heal-book,
A task-book of infinite roots.

November 1933

Стихи памяти Андрея Белого

Голубые глаза и горячая лобная кость —
Мировая манила тебя молодящая злость.

И за то, что тебе суждена была чудная власть,
Положили тебя никогда не судить и не клясть.

На тебя надевали тиару — юрода колпак,
Бирюзовый учитель, мучитель, властитель, дурак!

Как снежок, на Москве заводил кавардак гоголёк, —
Непонятен-понятен, невнятен, запутан, лего́к…

Собиратель пространства, экзамены сдавший птенец,
Сочинитель, щеглёнок, студентик, студент, бубенец.

Конькобежец и первенец, веком гонимый взашей
Под морозную пыль образуемых вновь падежей.

Часто пишется — казнь, а читается правильно — песнь.
Может быть, простота — уязвимая смертью болезнь?

Прямизна нашей мысли не только пугач для детей?
Не бумажные дести, а вести спасают людей.

Как стрекозы садятся, не чуя воды, в камыши,
Налетели на мёртвого жирные карандаши.

На коленях держали для славных потомков листы,
Рисовали, просили прощенья у каждой черты.

Меж тобой и страной ледяная рождается связь —
Так лежи, молодей и лежи, бесконечно прямясь.

Да не спросят тебя молодые, грядущие — те,
Каково тебе там — в пустоте, в чистоте-сироте…

10–11 января 1934

To the Memory of Andrei Bely

Blue eyes and a burning forehead bone unfurled—
You were lured by a young fury of the world.

Since in the magic power you were so well versed,
You should never be judged or cursed.

They gave you a tiara—a jester's cap and bells for a crown,
A turquoise teacher, a torturer, a ruler, a clown.

A little Gogolish snowstorm, you strutted along a Moscow street,
Implausibly plausible, entangled and light, indiscrete . . .

Space assembler, a fledgling that passed his exams, a prudent
Schoolboy, an author, a goldfinch nestling, a bell-ringer, a student.

An ice-skater, a first-born of the age which drove you out into spaces
Filled with an icy dust of newly-formed declensions and cases.

Often, we spell "malady" but say "melody" at ease.
Perhaps simplicity is just a mortal disease?

Is our forthright thought just meant to scare the children away?
It's by the news, not rims of paper, that people are saved.

Like dragonflies missing the water land in the reeds,
The fat pencils attack the deceased.

On their knees they held pages for our glorious future ages,
Begging to forgive them for every line, those sages.

An icy bond is born between your country and you—
So, lie down getting younger, forever upright and new.

Let those young future offspring never dare
Ask you, a pure orphan, how you feel in the void over there.

January 10–11, 1934

Утро 10 января 1934

1

Меня преследуют две-три случайных фразы, —
Весь день твержу: печаль моя жирна.
О Боже, как жирны и синеглазы
Стрекозы смерти, как лазурь черна…

Где первородство? Где счастливая повадка?
Где плавкий ястребок на самом дне очей?
Где вежество? Где горькая украдка?
Где ясный стан? Где прямизна речей,

Запутанных, как честные зигзаги
У конькобежца в пламень голубой,
Когда скользит, исполненный отваги,
С голуботвёрдой чокаясь рекой?

Он дирижировал кавказскими горами
И, машучи, ступал на тесных Альп тропы,
И, озираючись, пустынными брегами
Шёл, чуя разговор бесчисленной толпы.

Толпы умов, влияний, впечатлений
Он перенёс, как лишь могущий мог:
Рахиль глядела в зеркало явлений,
А Лия пела и плела венок.

The Morning of January 10, 1934

1

I am haunted by a couple of random phrases:
"My grief is rich in fat,"* I utter all day long.
Oh, God, those dragonflies of death have such blue eyes,
So fat they are, so black is the azure of the skies.

Where's the right of the first-born? Where's the joy of rite?
Where's a nestling of the hawk on the deep bottom of the eyes?
Where's knowledge? The bitter taste of a secret insight?
Where's the clear posture? Where's the candor of speeches

Entangled like the ice-skater's honest zigzags
And mingled with a blue fire when he bravely glides
Clinking with a hard-blue icy river crust,
Being whirled in a frosty thrust?

He conducted the orchestra of the Caucasian mounts,
Waving his hands, stepped onto the Alpine steep paths,
And looking back at the deserted shores,
He went on grasping the talk of countless crowds.

A mighty mind, he carried on a throng
Of minds, impressions, and effects:
Rachel looked into the mirror of events
While Leah weaved a wreath and sang a song.

---

*   A remake of "my grief is light," from Alexander Pushkin's "On Hills of Georgia" (1829).

2

Когда душе столь то́ропкой, столь робкой
Предстанет вдруг событий глубина,
Она бежит виющеюся тропкой —
Но смерти ей тропина не ясна.

Он, кажется, дичился умиранья
Застенчивостью славной новичка
Иль звука-первенца в блистательном собраньи,
Что льётся внутрь в продольный лес смычка.

И льётся вспять, ещё ленясь и мерясь,
То мерой льна, то мерой волокна,
И льётся смолкой, сам себе не верясь,
Из ничего, из нити, из темна,

Лиясь для ласковой, только что снятой маски,
Для пальцев гипсовых, не держащих пера,
Для укрупнённых губ, для укреплённой ласки
Крупнозернистого покоя и добра.

3

Дышали шуб меха. Плечо к плечу теснилось.
Кипела киноварь здоровья, кровь и пот.
Сон в оболочке сна, внутри которой снилось
На полшага продвинуться вперёд.

А посреди толпы стоял гравировальщик,
Готовый перенесть на истинную медь
То, что обугливший бумагу рисовальщик
Лишь крохоборствуя успел запечатлеть.

Как будто я повис на собственных ресницах,
И созревающий, и тянущийся весь, —
Доколе не сорвусь — разыгрываю в лицах
Единственное, что мы знаем днесь.

16–22 января 1934

2

When a soul, impatient, shy and fast
Suddenly sees the things to their depth,
She rushes along the winding path,
Not seeing clearly the way of death.

He seemed to shy away from dying
With a sweet shyness of a novice
Or like the first-born sound
In brilliant chords flows bound

To the stretched wood of a bow string,
Flows back and forth, idling and measuring
With the measure of flax or fiber, or like resin,
Flows out of nowhere, from thread, amazed,

From dark onto a tender newly-cast mask,
For the plaster fingers holding no pen,
For the enlarged lips and mighty caress
Of large coarse-grained goodness and peace.

3

The furs of coats breathed. Shoulder to shoulder squeezed.
The cinnabar of health boiled with blood and sweat:
A dream was wrapped in a dream, the dream inside
Was dreaming to move on—half a step ahead.

An engraver stood amidst the crowd, midway,
Ready to transfer onto a true bronze plate
What a draftsman managed to portray
Blackening the paper with petty lines of late.

As if I were hanging on my own eyelashes
Ripening, stretching until I finally fall down,—
I am acting all the parts in the same play
Presenting the only thing we know today.

January 16–22, 1934

10 января 1934 *(вариант 2)*

Памяти Андрея Белого

Меня преследуют две-три случайных фразы, —
Весь день твержу: печаль моя жирна.
О Боже, как жирны и синеглазы
Стрекозы смерти, как лазурь черна . . .

Где первородство? Где счастливая повадка?
Где плавкий ястребок на самом дне очей?
Где вежество? Где горькая украдка?
Где ясный стан? Где прямизна речей,

Запутанных, как честные зигзаги
У конькобежца в пламень голубой,
Железный пух в морозной крутят тяге
С голуботвёрдой чокаясь рекой?

Ему солей трехъярусных растворы
И мудрецов германских голоса
И русских первенцев блистательные споры
Представились в полвека, в полчаса.

И вдруг открылась музыка в засаде,
Уже не хищницей лиясь из-под смычков,
Не ради слуха или неги ради —
Лиясь для мышц и бьющихся висков.

Лиясь для ласковой, только что снятой маски,
Для пальцев гипсовых, не держащих пера,
Для укрупнённых губ, для укреплённой ласки
Крупнозернистого покоя и добра.

January 10, 1934 *(version 2)*

To the Memory of Andrei Bely

I am haunted by a couple of random phrases:
"My grief is rich in fat," I utter all day long.
Oh, God, those dragonflies of death have such blue eyes,
So fat they are, so black is the azure of the skies . . .

Where is the right of the first-born? Where's the joy of rite?
Where is a nestling of the hawk on the deep bottom of the eyes?
Where is knowledge? The bitter taste of a secret insight?
Where's a clear posture? Where's the candor of speeches

Entangled as the ice-skater's honest zigzags
And mingled with a blue fire as if
An iron fluff were whirled in a frosty thrust
Clinking with a hard-blue icy river crust?

He grasped as if in half an hour, half an age,
Solutions of three-layered salts,
The voices of German sages
And brilliant disputes of Russian first-born sons.

Suddenly the music rushed from ambush, ample,
But not as a predator leaping from the bow-strings,
Not to delight and not to please the ear—
But as balm for the muscles and each struggling temple,

Flowing for a tender newly-cast mask,
For the plaster fingers holding no pen,
For enlarged lips and mighty caress
Of large coarse-grained goodness and peace.

Дышали шуб меха, плечо к плечу теснилось,
Кипела киноварь здоровья, кровь и пот.
Сон в оболочке сна, внутри которой снилось
На полшага продвинуться вперёд!

А посреди толпы стоял гравировальщик,
Готовясь перенесть на истинную медь
То, что обугливший бумагу рисовальщик
Лишь крохоборствуя успел запечатлеть.

Как будто я повис на собственных ресницах
И созревающий, и тянущийся весь —
Доколе не сорвусь — разыгрываю в лицах
Единственное, что мы знаем днесь.

16 января 1934

The furs of coats breathed, shoulder to shoulder, squeezed.
The cinnabar of health boiled with blood and sweat:
A dream was wrapped in a dream, the dream inside
Was dreaming to move on half a step ahead.

An engraver stood amidst the crowd, midway,
Preparing to transfer onto a true bronze plate
What a draftsmen managed to portray
Blackening the paper with petty lines of late.

As if I were hanging on my own eyelashes
Ripening, stretching until I'd finally fall down—
I am acting all the parts in the same play,
Presenting the only thing we learned today.

January 16, 1934

Из Воронежских тетрадей
(стихотворения 1935–1937)

Из Первой тетради

* * *

Пусти меня, отдай меня, Воронеж:
Уронишь ты меня иль проворонишь,
Ты выронишь меня или вернёшь,
Воронеж — блажь, Воронеж — ворон, нож…

апрель 1935

* * *

Я должен жить, хотя я дважды умер,
А город от воды ополоумел:
Как он хорош, как весел, как скуласт,
Как на лемех приятен жирный пласт,
Как степь лежит в апрельском провороте,
А небо, небо — твой Буонаротти…

апрель 1935

* * *

Лишив меня морей, разбега и разлёта
И дав стопе упор насильственной земли,
Чего добились вы? Блестящего расчёта —
Губ шевелящихся отнять вы не могли.

май 1935

From the Voronezh Notebooks
(poems of 1935–1937)

From the First Notebook

* * *

Let go, Voronezh, raven-town,
Let me be, don't let me down,
You'll drop me, crop me, won't revive,
Voronezh—whim, Voronezh—raven, knife . . .

April 1935

* * *

I have to live though I died twice
While the water made the city crazy here:
With high cheek-bones, it is so joyous,
And the ploughshare likes its fat layer,
How in its April's turnover the steppe lies,
And like Buonarotti's are the skies . . .

April 1935

* * *

Having deprived me of seas, flight, and space,
You gave me a foothold of a forcible land,
What have you gained? A brilliant end:
You failed to take my moving lips away.

May 1935

* * *

День стоял о пяти головах. Сплошные пять суток
Я, сжимаясь, гордился пространством за то, что росло на дрожжах.
Сон был больше, чем слух, слух был старше, чем сон, — слитен, чуток,
А за нами неслись большаки на ямщицких вожжах.

День стоял о пяти головах, и, чумея от пляса,
Ехала конная, пешая шла черноверхая масса —
Расширеньем аорты могущества в белых ночах — нет, в ножах —
Глаз превращался в хвойное мясо.

На вершок бы мне синего моря, на игольное только ушко,
Чтобы двойка конвойного времени парусами неслась хорошо.
Сухомятная русская сказка, деревянная ложка, ау!
Где вы, трое славных ребят из железных ворот ГПУ?

Чтобы Пушкина чудный товар не пошёл по рукам дармоедов,
Грамотеет в шинелях с наганами племя пушкиноведов —
Молодые любители белозубых стишков,
На вершок бы мне синего моря, на игольное только ушко!

Поезд шёл на Урал. В раскрытые рты нам
Говорящий Чапаев с картины скакал звуковой —
За бревенчатым тылом, на ленте простынной
Утонуть и вскочить на коня своего.

апрель–1 июня 1935

* * *

The day was five-headed: five unbreakable days.
Shrinking, I grew proud of space rising on yeast.
Sleep was larger than hearing, which was older than sleep,
Solid but alert, and the road rushed behind us pulled
                              by the coachman's reins.

The day stood five-headed, and crazy from its dance,
The black mass moved on horses, on foot, and in trance
The might of white nights made the aorta expand—no, of five knives—
And the eye turned into coniferous flesh.

If I had been given an inch of blue sea, just an eye of a needle,
So that a double-boat of escorted time sailed along fast and well.
Dry food of the Russian fairy tale, a wooden spoon, hey, you!
Where are you, three nice guys from the iron gates of the GPU?

Young lovers of white-teeth verses are learning to read,
A young tribe of Pushkin scholars in uniforms and with guns,
So that Pushkin's fine goods are not stolen by the spongers indeed.
If I had been given an inch of blue sea, just an eye of a needle!

The train moved to the Urals. Talking Chapayev* galloped
From a sound film-track right into our open mouths, a sight to be seen—
To drown in the river and mount his horse back properly propped
Behind a wooden rear, a white sheet of the screen.

April–June 1, 1935

---

*   A movie about Chapayev, a Red Army commander killed in an ambush prepared by the
      White Army during the civil war, was one of the most popular films of the 1930s.

* * *

Ещё мы жизнью по́лны в высшей мере,
Ещё гуляют в городах Союза
Из мотыльковых, лапчатых материй
Китайчатые платьица и блузы.

Ещё машинка номер первый едко
Каштановые собирает взятки,
И падают на чистую салфетку
Разумные, густеющие прядки.

Ещё стрижей довольно и касаток,
Ещё комета нас не очумила,
И пишут звездоносно и хвостато
Толковые, лиловые чернила.

24 мая 1935

* * *

Римских ночей полновесные слитки,
Юношу Гёте манившее лоно —
Пусть я в ответе, но не в убытке:
Есть многодонная жизнь вне закона.

июнь 1935

* * *

We are still sentenced to life,
Chinese blouses and gowns
From a butterfly moth-like textile
Still stroll along the Soviet towns.

A hair-cutter number one
Still collects chestnut bribes,
And smart dark curls fall down
On a clean white napkin in piles.

There are still enough swifts and swallows,
A comet hasn't plagued us as of now,
And intelligent purple ink follows
It with starry tails and pens it down.

May 24, 1935

* * *

Solid gold bars of the Roman nights—
A bosom that lured young Goethe:
I am accountable, but I haven't lost:
There is a fathomless life of outlaws.

June 1935

* * *

За Паганини длиннопалым
Бегут цыганскою гурьбой —
Кто с чохом — чех, кто с польским балом,
А кто с венгерской чемчурой.

Девчонка, выскочка, гордячка,
Чей звук широк, как Енисей, —
Утешь меня игрой своей —
На голове твоей, полячка,
Марины Мнишек холм кудрей,
Смычок твой мнителен, скрипачка.

Утешь меня Шопеном чалым,
Серьёзным Брамсом, нет, постой —
Парижем мощно-одичалым,
Мучным и потным карнавалом
Иль брагой Вены молодой —

Вертлявой, в дирижерских фрачках,
В дунайских фейерверках, скачках,
И вальс из гроба в колыбель
Переливающей, как хмель.

Играй же на разрыв аорты
С кошачьей головой во рту!
Три чёрта было, ты — четвёртый,
Последний, чудный чёрт в цвету!

5 апреля–июль 1935

* * *

They run like a gypsy throng
After the long-fingered Paganini—all:
Some with Czech checkers all along,
Hungarian boche hunger, or a Polish ball.

Console me with your play,
A girl, upstart and proud,
Your sound is as wide as the Yenisei,
A Pole, your head is a mount
Of Marina Mnishek's curls,
Fiddler, your bow is fickle as well.

Console me with your open Chopin,
With serious Brahms, no, wait—
With Paris powerfully wild,
A carnival full of sweet and sweat,
Or with Vienna's young brew—

Fidgeting in conductor's tails,
All in the Danube's fireworks, races,
From a grave to a cradle
Pouring a waltz-like wine.

So play to the rapture of aorta
With a cat's head in your mouth!
There were three devils, you're the fourth,
The last, marvelous colorful sprite!

April 5–July 1935

* * *

Исполню дымчатый обряд:
В опале предо мной лежат
Морского лета земляники —
Двуискренние сердолики
И муравьиный брат — агат,
Но мне милей простой солдат
Морской пучины — серый, дикий,
Которому никто не рад.

июль 1935

* * *

I'll fulfill a dim rite:
Summer strawberries lie
In opal casings before me—
Sards with double souls
And an ant's brother, agate,
But dearer to me is rank and file
Of the sea depth—a gray, wild
Soldier whom no one likes.

July 1935

Из Второй тетради

* * *

Не у меня, не у тебя — у них
Вся сила окончаний родовых:
Их воздухом поющ тростник и скважист,
И с благодарностью улитки губ людских
Потянут на себя их дышащую тяжесть.
Нет имени у них. Войди в их хрящ,
И будешь ты наследником их княжеств, —

И для людей, для их сердец живых,
Блуждая в их извилинах, развивах,
Изобразишь и наслажденья их,
И то, что мучит их — в приливах и отливах.

9–27 декабря 1936

From the Second Notebook

* * *

Not I, not you—but they
Have all the power of the gender endings:
A porous reed is singing with their air,
The snails of human lips will gratefully inhale
Their breathing heaviness. They are
Unnamed. Go into their cartilages—
And you'll inherit their kingdoms then,—

Wandering in curves and windings,
You'll show the human kind
And human living hearts
How they enjoy and strive—in ebbs and tidings.

December 9–27, 1936

* * *

Улыбнись, ягнёнок гневный с Рафаэлева холста, —
На холсте уста вселенной, но она уже не та...

В лёгком воздухе свирели раствори жемчужин боль —
В синий, синий цвет синели океана въелась соль...

Цвет воздушного разбоя и пещерной густоты,
Складки бурного покоя на коленях разлиты.

На скале черствее хлеба — молодых тростинки рощ,
И плывёт углами неба восхитительная мощь.

9 января 1937

* * *

Smile, angry lamb from Rafael's canvas, don't rage*—
The lips of the Universe are there, but the world has changed:

In the syrinx's light air, you dissolve the pain of pearls—
Salt has eaten up the ocean's azure, lazuline sapphire light.

The hue of airy banditry and the density of the cave,
The pleats of the stormy peace on her knees and lap are spread.

The reeds of the young groves on the rock staler than bread,
But in the corners of the sky floats an amazing might.

January 9, 1937

---

*   The painting that inspired Osip Mandelstam in his Voronezh exile was Rafael's "The Holy
Family with a Lamb" (1507): https://www.raphaelsanzio.org/The-Holy-Family-With-A-
Lamb-1507.html.

* * *

Дрожжи мира дорогие:
Звуки, слёзы и труды —
Ударенья дождевые
Закипающей беды,
И потери звуковые
Из какой вернуть руды?

В нищей памяти впервые
Чуешь вмятины слепые,
Медной полные воды, —
И идёшь за ними следом,
Сам себе немил, неведом —
И слепой, и поводырь . . .

12–18 января 1937

* * *

Ещё не умер ты. Ещё ты не один,
Покуда с нищенкой-подругой
Ты наслаждаешься величием равнин,
И мглой, и холодом, и вьюгой.

В роскошной бедности, в могучей нищете
Живи спокоен и утешен —
Благословенны дни и ночи те,
И сладкогласный труд безгрешен.

Несчастлив тот, кого, как тень его,
Пугает лай и ветер косит,
И жалок тот, кто, сам полуживой,
У тени милостыню просит.

15–16 января 1937

* * *

World's golden yeast, our dear
Sounds, labors, and tears—
Rainy accents foaming
Of a boiling grief,
From which ore can one
Sound losses retrieve?

In your pauper memory
For the first time you feel
Bronze water in blind dents,—
You follow blindly their trail,
Unknown to yourself, unkind,
Both the blind and the guide.

January 12–18, 1937

* * *

You haven't died yet. You are not alone
While with a pauper girlfriend
You delight in the magnificence of the plains,
With a blizzard, gloom, and cold.

In luxurious poverty, in a mighty need
Live peacefully, consoled:
Blessed are those days and nights,
And your sweet melodious labor is sacred.

Unhappy is he who like his shadow
Is scared by the barking and is cut down by wind,
And wretched is he who half alive himself
Is begging alms from ghouls.

January 15–16, 1937

* * *

Что делать нам с убитостью равнин,
С протяжным голодом их чуда?
Ведь то, что мы открытостью их мним,
Мы сами видим, засыпая, зрим —
И всё растёт вопрос: куда они, откуда,
И не ползёт ли медленно по ним
Тот, о котором мы во сне кричим, —
Народов будущих Иуда?*

16 января 1937

---

*   Н. Я. Мандельштам считала строку «Пространств несозданных Иуда?» цензурированным вариантом и предлагала «Народов будущих Иуда». Н. Я. Мандельштам, «Комментарий к стихам 1930-1937 гг.» // «Жизнь и творчество О. Э. Мандельштама» (Воронеж: Изд-во Воронежского университета, 1990), 282.

* * *

What should we do with murdered plains,
With a prolonged hunger of their wonder?
For what seems their openness to us,
Drowsing, we see in dreams, hallucinations—
The question grows: where are they from, whence,
Isn't the one slowly crawling there,
The one who scares us to crying in a nightmare—
Isn't he Judas of the future nations?*

January 16, 1937

---

* Nadezhda Mandelstam considered the line "Judas of the unformed spaces" a "censored" version and suggested instead "Isn't he Judas of the future nations?" See Nadezhda Mandel'shtam, "Kommentarii k stikham 1930–1937 gg.," 282.

* * *

Вооружённый зреньем узких ос,
Сосущих ось земную, ось земную,
Я чую всё, с чем свидеться пришлось,
И вспоминаю наизусть и всуе . . .

И не рисую я, и не пою,
И не вожу смычком черноголосым:
Я только в жизнь впиваюсь и люблю
Завидовать могучим, хитрым осам.

О, если б и меня когда-нибудь могло
Заставить, сон и смерть минуя,
Стрекало воздуха и летнее тепло
Услышать ось земную, ось земную . . .

8 февраля 1937

* * *

Armed with the vision of narrow wasps
Sucking the axis of the earth, the earth,
I feel and hear all I've had to watch
And recollect by heart—in vain, alas . . .

I neither paint nor sing,
Nor do I run a black-voiced bow across the strings—
I just sting into life and love
To envy mighty cunning wasps.

Oh, if an air's barb and summer warmth
Could help me to avoid both sleep and death
And could have made me hear hence
The axis of the earth, the axis of the earth . . .

February 8, 1937

Из Третьей тетради

Стихи о неизвестном солдате

Этот воздух пусть будет свидетелем,
Дальнобойное сердце его,
И в землянках всеядный и деятельный
Океан без окна — вещество . . .

До чего эти звёзды изветливы!
Все им нужно глядеть — для чего?
В осужденье судьи и свидетеля,
В океан без окна, вещество.

Помнит дождь, неприветливый сеятель, —
Безымянная манна его, —
Как лесистые крестики метили
Океан или клин боевой.

Будут люди холодные, хилые
Убивать, холодать, голодать
И в своей знаменитой могиле
Неизвестный положен солдат.

Научи меня, ласточка хилая,
Разучившаяся летать,
Как мне с этой воздушной могилой
Без руля и крыла совладать.

И за Лермонтова Михаила
Я отдам тебе строгий отчёт,
Как сутулого учит могила
И воздушная яма влечёт.

From the Third Notebook

Verses on the Unknown Soldier

Let this air be our eyewitness,
His long-range beating heart,
In the dug-outs— active, omnivorous
Substance—a windowless ocean strives hard . . .

How sneaky these stars are! In commotion,
They would peep and watch—for what purpose?
Into the substance, the windowless ocean,
To convict the judge and the witness.

Rain, a dreary sower and stark, —
Its nameless manna remembers
How a forest of crosses marked
The ocean or a fighting file's members.

Sickly, freezing men
Will kill, chill, and starve,
And an unknown soldier then
Will be laid in his famous grave.

A sickly swallow unable to fly,
Teach me: how can I
Cope with that airy grave
Without a rudder or sails?

And I will give you a strict account
For Lermontov Mikhail—how
A hunchback is taught by the grave,
While an air-hole lures and hauls.

Шевелящимися виноградинами
Угрожают нам эти миры
И висят городами украденными,
Золотыми обмолвками, ябедами,
Ядовитого холода ягодами —
Растяжимых созвездий шатры,
Золотые созвездий жиры . . .

Сквозь эфир десятично-означенный
Свет размолотых в луч скоростей
Начинает число, опрозраченный
Светлой болью и молью нулей.

И за полем полей поле новое
Треугольным летит журавлём,
Весть летит светопыльной обновою,
И от битвы вчерашней светло.

Весть летит светопыльной обновою:
— Я не Лейпциг, я не Ватерлоо,
Я не Битва Народов, я новое,
От меня будет свету светло.

Аравийское месиво, крошево,
Свет размолотых в луч скоростей,
И своими косыми подошвами
Луч стоит на сетчатке моей.

Миллионы убитых задёшево
Протоптали тропу в пустоте, —
Доброй ночи! всего им хорошего
От лица земляных крепостей!

Неподкупное небо окопное —
Небо крупных оптовых смертей, —
За тобой, от тебя, целокупное,
Я губами несусь в темноте —

These worlds threaten us
With stirring hanging grapes,
And the tents of stretched constellations
Hang like stolen cities and towns,
Golden hints and denunciations,
Berries of poisonous cold,
Constellations of fatty gold.

Through the ether of ten-digit zeroes
The light of speeds ground down to a beam
Starts a number, made lucent and clear
By the bright pain of holes and moles.

And beyond the field of fields a new battlefield
Flies like a triangular flock of cranes,
The news flies like a new dust-like light,
And it's bright from the yesterday's fight.

The news flies like a light-dust novelty:
—I am not Leipzig, not Waterloo,
Not the Battle of Nations—I am new,
I will dazzle the world with my light.

Arabian mess, mash and hash,
The light of speeds ground down to a ray—
And trampling my retina with its squint soles,
The beam flattens the pupil of my eye.

The millions of murdered cheaply, wholesale
Have trampled a path in the void—
Good night, good sleep to them all
On behalf of the dug-out forts!

Incorruptible heaven of trenches,
The sky of deaths, wholesale and large-scale—
Beyond you, from you, the whole one,
I fly on my lips in the dark—

За воронки, за насыпи, осыпи,
По которым он медлил и мглил:
Развороченных — пасмурный, оспенный
И приниженный гений могил.

Хорошо умирает пехота,
И поёт хорошо хор ночной
Над улыбкой приплюснутой Швейка,
И над птичьим копьём Дон-Кихота,
И над рыцарской птичьей плюсной.

И дружи́т с человеком калека —
Им обоим найдётся работа,
И стучит по околицам века
Костылей деревянных семейка, —
Эй, товарищество, шар земной!

Для того ль должен череп развиться
Во весь лоб — от виска до виска, —
Чтоб в его дорогие глазницы
Не могли не вливаться войска?

Развивается череп от жизни
Во весь лоб — от виска до виска, —
Чистотой своих швов он дразни́т себя,
Понимающим куполом яснится,
Мыслью пенится, сам себе снится, —
Чаша чаш и отчизна отчизне,
Звёздным рубчиком шитый чепец,
Чепчик счастья — Шекспира отец . . .

Ясность ясеневая, зоркость яворовая
Чуть-чуть красная мчится в свой дом,
Словно обмороками затоваривая
Оба неба с их тусклым огнём.

Past the shell holes, mounds and mudslides,
Mayhem, where he lingered in haze:
Gloomy, pockmarked and humiliated genius
Of ingenious overturned graves.

The infantry dies nicely,
And nicely sings the nightly choir,
At Corporal Švejk's flattened smile,
At Don Quixote's bird-shaped spear,
And at birdlike visor of a knight.

And the cripple makes friends with a man,
There is work for both of them there:
The family of wooden crutches goes on
Knocking around the century's outskirts—
Hey, comradery—an earthly globe!

Should the skull develop its brow
Wide and high—from temple to temple,
So that the troops cannot but flow
Flooding its eyes—dear apples?

The skull develops through life
Along the whole brow—from temple to temple—
It tempts itself with the purity of its joints,
Shines with an intelligent dome,
Foams with thought, dreams of itself,
A cup of cups, homeland's home—
A cap sewn with a starry seam,
Shakespeare's father—a cap of joy . . .

Ash-tree's clarity, sycamore's keen sight
Rushes home, slightly tinted in red,
As if casting a spell of faint
On both skies with their pale light.

Нам союзно лишь то, что избыточно,
Впереди не провал, а промер,
И бороться за воздух прожиточный —
Эта слава другим не в пример.

И сознанье свое затоваривая
Полуобморочным бытиём,
Я ль без выбора пью это варево,
Свою голову ем под огнём?

Для того ль заготовлена тара
Обаянья в пространстве пустом,
Чтобы белые звёзды обратно
Чуть-чуть красные мчались в свой дом?

Слышишь, мачеха звёздного табора,
Ночь, что будет сейчас и потом?

Наливаются кровью аорты,
И звучит по рядам шепотком:
— Я рождён в девяносто четвёртом,
— Я рождён в девяносто втором . . . —
И в кулак зажимая истёртый
Год рожденья — с гурьбой и гуртом
Я шепчу обескровленным ртом:
— Я рождён в ночь с второго на третье
Января в девяносто одном
Ненадёжном году — и столетья
Окружают меня огнём.

1–15 марта 1937

Only abundance is our ally,
The depth to be fathomed, not abyss ahead,
And to fight for our ration of air
Is the glory beyond compare.

Having packed my own mind
With my fainting being,
Can I stop drinking this brew,
Eating my own head under fire?

Is the packaging of charm stored
In the empty space so that white stars
Should rush home slightly tinted in red?
A stepmother of a starry gypsy camp,

Do you hear, the night,
What will happen then from now on?

Aortas are flooded with blood,
And a whisper spreads through the ranks:
—"I was born in the year ninety-four,
—I was born in the year ninety-two . . ."
And squeezing in my fist
                          a worn-out date of my birth,
With bloodless lips I whisper amid crowd and herd:
"I was born on the night from the second to the third
Of January in the unreliable year
Of ninety-one, and centuries
Encircle me with fire."

March 1–15, 1937

* * *

Я молю, как жалости и милости,
Франция, твоей земли и жимолости,

Правды горлинок твоих и кривды карликовых
Виноградарей в их разгородках марлевых . . .

В лёгком декабре твой воздух стриженый
Индевеет — денежный, обиженный...

Но фиалка и в тюрьме — с ума сойти в безбрежности! —
Свищет песенка — насмешница, небрежница,

Где бурлила, королей смывая,
Улица июльская кривая . . .

А теперь в Париже, в Шартре, в Арле
Государит добрый Чаплин Чарли —

В океанском котелке с растерянною точностью
На шарнирах он куражится с цветочницей . . .

Там, где с розой на груди в двухбашенной испарине
Паутины каменеет шаль,

Жаль, что карусель воздушно-благодарная
Оборачивается, городом дыша, —

Наклони свою шею, безбожница
С золотыми глазами козы,

И кривыми картавыми ножницами
Купы скаредных роз раздразни.

3 марта 1937

* * *

I beg like compassion and grace,
Your land and honeysuckle, France,

The truth of your doves and the lies of dwarf makers of vines
With their gauze-like divides . . .

Your brushed air in a mild December
Freezes—money-seeking and offended . . .

But there's a violet even in jail: one can lose head in this infinity!—
A careless mocker, a song, still whistles light-heartedly,

Where a July curved street
Boiled, sweeping kings, like deadbeat...

And now in Paris, Chartres, Arles
There is a new king—Chaplin Charles:

With a flower girl he swaggers and fidgets
In an ocean bowler hat, with a perplexed precision on hinges . . .

It's a shame that an aerial grateful carousel
Turns back inhaling the whole town—

Where the shawl of a cobweb turns into stone
Sweating with its double towers—

Turn your neck, a godless beauty
With golden goatish eyes,

And tease the clumps of stingy roses
With curved guttural scissors.

March 3, 1937

* * *

Я скажу это начерно, шёпотом —
Потому что ещё не пора:
Достигается пóтом и опытом
Безотчётного неба игра . . .

И под временным небом чистилища
Забываем мы часто о том,
Что счастливое небохранилище —
Раздвижной и прижизненный дом.

9 марта 1937

* * *

I will say it in draft and in whisper
Since the time has not come yet:
The game of the instinctive heaven
Is attained through experience and sweat . . .

And beneath a temporal sky
Of purgatory we often forget
That this happy heaven's depot
Is our expanding and lifetime homestead.

March 9, 1937

* * *

Может быть, это точка безумия,
Может быть, это совесть твоя —
Узел жизни, в котором мы узнаны
И развязаны для бытия . . .

Так соборы кристаллов сверхжизненных
Добросовестный свет-паучок,
Распуская на рёбра, их сызнова
Собирает в единый пучок.

Чистых линий пучки благодарные,
Направляемы тихим лучом,
Соберутся, сойдутся когда-нибудь,
Словно гости с открытым челом,
Только здесь — на земле, а не на́ небе,
Как в наполненный музыкой дом, —
Только их не спугнуть, не изранить бы —
Хорошо, если мы доживём...

То, что я говорю, мне прости . . .
Тихо-тихо его мне прочти . . .

15 марта 1937

* * *

It might be the point of insanity,
It may be your consciousness as well:
This knot of life, in which we are
Singled out and untied for life . . .

Thus, a diligent spider, light
Disperses cathedrals of perpetual crystals
Upon the ribs of an arc and then
Gathers them into one beam again.

Led by a quiet ray,
Grateful beams of pure lines
Will gather one day,
Like frank friendly guests at table—
Only here, on earth, not in heaven,
As in the house full of music, able,
No one should hurt them or frighten—
Oh, if we could live to see it . . .

Forgive me what I have said
And quietly recite and re-read.

March 15, 1937

* * *

Не сравнивай: живущий несравним.
С каким-то ласковым испугом
Я согласился с равенством равнин,
И неба круг мне был недугом.

Я обращался к воздуху-слуге,
Ждал от него услуги или вести,
И собирался в путь, и плавал по дуге
Неначинающихся путешествий . . .

Где больше неба мне — там я бродить готов,
И ясная тоска меня не отпускает
От молодых ещё воронежских холмов
К всечеловеческим, яснеющим в Тоскане.

16 марта 1937

* * *

A living man's unique: do not compare.
I have accepted the equality of plains
With a somewhat tenderly scare
And was sick with a circle of the sky.

I summoned my true servant, air
Expecting services or news to get,
And having set my sail, I sailed along
The arc of voyages that never started yet . . .

I am eager to wander in the places where
There's more sky, but a serene sorrow
Doesn't let me go from young Voronezh hills
To those of Tuscany that illumine mankind.

March 16, 1937

* * *

Чтоб, приятель и ветра и капель,
Сохранил их песчаник внутри,
Нацарапали множество цапель
И бутылок в бутылках цари.

Украшался отборной собачиной
Египтян государственный стыд,
Мертвецов наделял всякой всячиной
И торчит пустячком пирамид.

То ли дело любимец мой кровный,
Утешительно-грешный певец,
Ещё слышен твой скрежет зубовный,
Беззаботного праха истец.

Размотавший на два завещанья
Слабовольных имуществ клубок
И в прощаньи отдав, в верещаньи,
Мир, который как череп глубок, —

Рядом с готикой жил озоруючи
И плевал на паучьи права
Наглый школьник и ангел ворующий,
Несравненный Виллон Франсуа.

Он разбойник небесного клира,
Рядом с ним не зазорно сидеть —
И пред самой кончиною мира
Будут жаворонки звенеть . . .

18 марта 1937

* * *

To help a friend of rain and wind
Save his sandstone within,
The kings scrawled a lot of herons
And bottles in their vessels.

Egyptians' state shame
Was adorned with a chosen canine,
They gave odds and ends to the dead,
And the trifle of pyramids still sticks out.

How much better is my favorite friend,
A sinful singer, consoler, my kin:
Your gritting teeth are still heard,
The plaintiff of careless dust.

He unwound for two testaments
A roll of his ill-willed assets,
And departing, gave us with a thrill
The world as deep as a skull—

Spitting at the spider's rights,
An impudent scholar, a stealing angel,
Played rough tricks near Gothic sites
Unrivaled Villon François.

He is a heavenly robber,
It is not shameful to sit near him:
Skylarks will still ring and warble
Before the end of the world . . .

March 18, 1937

* * *

Гончарами велик остров синий —
Крит зелёный. Запёкся их дар
В землю звонкую. Слышишь подземных
Плавников могучий удар?

Это море легко на помине
В осчастливленной обжигом глине,
И сосуда студёная власть
Раскололась на море и глаз.

Ты отдай мне моё, остров синий,
Крит летучий, отдай мне мой труд
И сосцами текучей богини
Воскорми обожжённый сосуд...

Это было и пелось, синея,
Много задолго до Одиссея,
До того, как еду и питьё
Называли «моя» и «моё».

Выздоравливай же, излучайся,
Волоокого неба звезда,
И летучая рыба — случайность,
И вода, говорящая «да».

21 марта 1937

* * *

A blue island, green Crete is extolled
For its potters. Their genius is baked
In the resonant soil. Can you hear
The mighty strike of the fins under the earth?

This sea is talk of the angels
In the clay blessed by the glaze,
And the vessel's glacial might
Is split into the sea and the eye.

Give me mine back, blue isle,
Winged Crete, give my toil back
And let a flowing goddess fertile
Breastfeed a glazed vessel's ache . . .

This was sung with a blue chime
Long before Odyssey's time,
Long before food and drink
were called "yours" and "mine."

Recover then, shine, illumine,
A star of the ox-eyed sky,
And a flying fish is just an instance,
So is water saying "yes."

March 1937

* * *

Длинной жажды должник виноватый,
Мудрый сводник вина и воды:
На боках твоих пляшут козлята
И под музыку зреют плоды.

Флейты свищут, клевещут и злятся,
Что беда на твоём ободу
Чёрно-красном, — и некому взяться
За тебя, чтоб поправить беду.

21 марта 1937

* * *

A guilty debtor of a long-time thirst,
A wise procurer of water and wine:
Goat's kids are frolicking on your sides,
And fruits ripen to the music tune.

The flutes whistle, swear, and rage
That you bear mischief on your edge
Black and red,—and there is no one
To take you and your grief away.

March 21, 1937

* * *

О, как же я хочу,
Нечуемый никем,
Лететь вослед лучу,
Где нет меня совсем.

А ты в кругу лучись —
Другого счастья нет —
И у звезды учись
Тому, что значит свет.

И я тебе хочу
Сказать, что я шепчу,
Что шёпотом лучу
Тебя, дитя, вручу.

Он только тем и луч,
Он только тем и свет,
Что шёпотом могуч
И лепетом согрет.

27 марта 1937

* * *

Нереиды мои, нереиды!
Вам рыданья — еда и питьё,
Дочерям средиземной обиды
Состраданье обидно моё.

март 1937

* * *

Oh, how I madly crave,
Perceived by none at all,
To fly along the ray
With nothing of me left.

And you radiate in a ring,—
There is no other joy in life,—
And learn from a distant star
The meaning of light.

And I would like to tell
You what I in a whisper spell
That whispering I will
Give you to the ray, child.

I'll tell you why it's light,
It's a ray only because
The whisper is its might
And the murmur is its warmth.

March 27, 1937

* * *

My nereids, oh, my nereids!
Your sobbing's been your food and drink for so long,
How insulting my compassion is
To the daughters of the Mediterranean wrong.

March 1937

* * *

Флейты греческой тэта и йота —
Словно ей не хватало молвы, —
Неизваянная, без отчёта,
Зрела, маялась, шла через рвы …

И её невозможно покинуть,
Стиснув зубы, её не унять,
И в слова языком не продвинуть,
И губами её не разнять …

А флейтист не узнает покоя:
Ему кажется, что он один,
Что когда-то он море родное
Из сиреневых вылепил глин …

Звонким шёпотом честолюбивым,
Вспоминающих шёпотом губ
Он торопится быть бережливым,
Емлет звуки — опрятен и скуп …

Вслед за ним мы его не повто́рим,
Комья глины в ладонях моря
И когда я наполнился морем —
Мором стала мне мера моя …

И свои-то мне губы не любы,
И убийство на том же корню —
И невольно на убыль, на убыль
Равнодействие флейты клоню …

7 апреля 1937

* * *

Greek flute's theta and iota—
As if it hadn't enough fame—
Unmodeled, unaccountable, toiled,
Ripened, overcame trenches, untamed . . .

It's impossible to abandon it,
It can't be tamed by the clenched teeth,
It can't be forced into words by a tongue,
Nor can it be split by the lips . . .

And a flute player won't find his peace:
It seems to him that he is forlorn,
That once he modeled this sea
From lilac and serene clays . . .

With a resonant whisper of the ambitious,
Recollecting with whispering lips,
He hurries to be prudent and cautious
And relieves clear sounds, neat and crisp . . .

We can never repeat him, replay,
Molding lumps of clay in the palms,
And when I was filled up with the sea —
My own measure became my blight . . .

My own lips are not dear to me,
Murder is too from the same root,
And unconsciously I try to subdue,
To suppress the voice of the flute . . .

April 7, 1937

* * *

На меня нацелилась груша да черёмуха —
Силою рассыпчатой бьёт меня без промаха.

Кисти вместе с звёздами, звёзды вместе с кистями, —
Что за двоевластье там? В чьём соцветьи истина?

С цвету ли, с размаха ли — бьёт воздушно-целыми
В воздух, убиваемый кистенями белыми.

И двойного запаха сладость неуживчива:
Борется и тянется — смешана, обрывчива.

4 мая 1937

* * *

I'm under fire of a bird cherry tree and a pear tree—
Without missing their shrapnel fire hits me.

Constellations with bunches, clusters with stars—
Why the diarchy? In which inflorescence is the truth?

They shoot in full bloom or in full swing with whole-air:
White bunches or bludgeons are shaking the atmosphere.

While the sweetness of the double aroma from the start
Struggles and stretches, is mixed, torn apart.

May 4, 1937

* * *

[Стихи к Н<аталии> Е. Штемпель]

I

К пустой земле невольно припадая,
Неравномерной сладкою походкой
Она идёт — чуть-чуть опережая
Подругу быструю и юношу-погодка.
Её влечёт стеснённая свобода
Одушевляющего недостатка,
И, может статься, ясная догадка
В её походке хочет задержаться —
О том, что эта вешняя погода
Для нас — праматерь гробового свода,
И это будет вечно начинаться.

II

Есть женщины, сырой земле родные,
И каждый шаг их — гулкое рыданье,
Сопровождать воскресших и впервые
Приветствовать умерших — их призванье.
И ласки требовать от них преступно,
И расставаться с ними непосильно.
Сегодня — ангел, завтра — червь могильный,
А послезавтра — только очертанье...
Что было — поступь — станет недоступно...
Цветы бессмертны. Небо целокупно.
И всё, что будет, — только обещанье.

4 мая 1937

* * *

[Poems for N<atalia> E. Shtempel]

I

Unwillingly clinging to a bare land,
With an uneven sweet gait
She goes—a little bit ahead
Of a swift girlfriend and her young groom.
She is drawn by the constrained freedom
Of an uplifting imperfection.
Perhaps a clear prediction
Clings to her gait, longing to stay:
That this spring weather
Is for us a grave's foremother,
And this will begin forever.

II

Some women are kin to damp earth,
Their each step is a resonant dirge,
They are summoned to accompany
The risen and be the first to greet the dead.
It is a crime to demand for their caresses,
And it is impossible to leave them.
Today—an angel, tomorrow—a grave's worm,
And the next day—just a shadow . . .
What was a posture will be gone . . .
Flowers are immortal, the sky is wholesome,
And everything to come—is just a promise.

May 4, 1937

Abbreviations

ABC—Ezra Pound, *ABC of Reading* (New York: New Directions, 1987).

CPL—Osip Mandelstam, *The Complete Critical Prose and Letters*, ed. Jane Garry Harris, trans. J. G. Harris and Constance Link (Ann Arbor, MI: Ardis, 1979).

LE—Ezra Pound, *Literary Essays*, ed. T. S. Eliot (London: Faber & Faber, 1954).

Bibliography

Publications of Works by Osip E. Mandelstam

Mandel'shtam, Osip. *Kamen'* [Stone]. 1st edition. St. Petersburg: Acme, 1913.

——. *Kamen'* [Stone]. 2nd edition. St. Petersburg: Giperborei, 1916.

——. *Kamen'* [Stone]. Moscow and Petersburg: Gosizdat, 1923.

——. *Tristia*. Petrograd and Berlin: Petropolis, 1922.

——. *Stikhotvoreniia* [Poems]. Moscow and Leningrad: Gosizdat, 1928.

——. *Sobranie stikhotvorenii v dvukh tomakh* [Collected poems in two volumes]. Edited by G. Struve and B. Filippov. Washington and New York: Mezhdunarodnoe literaturnoe sodruzhestvo [International Literary Association], 1967.

——. *Sobranie stikhotvorenii v chetyrekh tomakh* [Collected poems in four volumes]. Edited by G. Struve and B. Filippov. Washington and New York: Mezhdunarodnoe literaturnoe sodruzhestvo [International Literary Association], 1967–1981.

——. *Stikhotvoreniia* [Poems]. Compiled by N. Khardzhiev. Leningrad: Sovetskii pisatel', 1973.

——. *Slovo i kul'tura* [Word and culture]. Moscow: Sovetskii pisatel', 1987.

——. *Sochineniia v dvukh tomakh* [Works in two volumes]. Edited by Pavel Nerler. Moscow: Khudozhestvennaia literatura, 1990.

——. *Stikhi. Perevody. Esse. Stat'i* [Poems. Translations. Essays. Articles]. Tbilisi: Merani, 1990.

——. *Sobranie stikhotvorenii v chetyrekh tomakh* [Collected poems in four volumes]. Edited by G. Struve and B. Filippov. Reprint ed. Moscow: Terra, 1991.

——. *Sobraniie sochinenii v chetyrekh tomakh* [Collected works in two volumes]. Edited by Pavel Nerler and Andrei Nikitaiev. Moscow: Khudozhestvennaia literatura, 1993–1997.

——. *Polnoe sobranie sochinenii i pisem* [Complete collected works and letters]. 3 vols. Compiled and edited by A. G. Mets. Moscow: Progress and Pleiada, 2010.

——. *Sobranie stikhotvorenii 1906–1937* [Collected poems 1906–1937]. Compiled by Oleg Lekmanov and Maksim Amelin. Moscow: Ruteniia, 2017.

Translations into English

Mandelstam, Osip. *The Complete Poetry of Osip Mandelstam*. Translated by Burton Raffel and Anna Burago. Albany, NY: State University of New York Press, 1973.

————*Selected Poems*. Translated by Clarence Brown and W. S. Merwin. New York: Atheneum, 1974.

————. *50 Poems*. Translated by Bernard Meares. Introduction by Joseph Brodsky. New York: Persea Books, 1977.

————. *Poems*. Translated by James Green. London: Elek Books, 1977.

————. *The Complete Critical Prose and Letters*. Edited by Jane Gary Harris Translated by J. G. Harris and Constance Link. Ann Arbor, MI: Ardis, 1979.

————. *Poems*. Translated by James Green. Revised and enlarged edition. London: Granada, 1980.

————. *Stone*. Translated and introduced by Robert Tracy. Princeton, NJ: Princeton University Press, 1981.

————. *Selected Poems*. Translated by David McDuff. London: Writers and Readers, 1983.

————. *Tristia*. Translated by Bruce McClelland. Barrytown, NY: Station Hill Press, 1987.

————. *Osip Mandelstam. New Translations*. Edited by Ilya Bernstein. New York: Ugly Duckling Presse, 2006.

————. *Modernist Archaist: Selected Poems*. With essay and translations by Kevin M. F. Platt. Translated by Charles Bernstein, Bernard Meyers, Clarence Brown, Eugene Ostashevsky, Kevin M. F. Platt, and W. S. Merwin. Culver City, CA: Whale & Star, 2008.

————. *Poems of Osip Mandelstam*. Translated by Peter France. New York: New Directions, 2014.

Translations of Osip Mandelstam's poems into other languages

Mandelstam, Osip. [Mandelstam, Ossip]. *Voyage en Arménie*. Translated by Claude B. Levenson. Lausanne, Switzerland: L'Age d'Homme, 1973.

————. *Tristia et autres poèmes*. Translated by François Kérel. Paris: Gallimard, 1975.

Die Dichtung Ossip Mandelstams. Der Meridian. Endfassung, Vorstufen, Materialien. Translated by Paul Celan. Frankfurt am Main: Suhrkamp, 1999.

Criticism

Bacigalupo, Massimo. *The Forméd Trace: The Later Poetry of Ezra Pound*. New York: Columbia University Press, 1980.

Bakhtin, Mikhail. "Problema soderzhaniia, materiala i formy v slovesnom khudozhestvennom tvorchestve" [The problem of content, material, and form in literary art]. In *Voprosy literatury i estetiki* [Questions of literature and esthetics]. Moscow: Khudozhestvennaia literatura, 1975.

Barnstone, Willis, ed. *Modern European Poetry.* Translated by Roger Shattuck. New York: Bantam Books, 1996.

Benjamin, Walter. "The Task of the Translator." In *Illuminations,* edited by Hanna Arendt, translated by Harry Zohn, 69–82. New York: Schocken Books, 1969.

Broyde, S. J. "Osip Mandelstam's 'Nasedsij Podkovu.'" In *Slavic Poetics: Essays in Honor of Kiril Taranovsky,* edited by Roman Jakobson, C. H. van Schooneveld, and Dean S. Worth, 49–66. Paris: Mouton, 1973.

Bush, Ronald. "Late Cantos LXXII–CXVII." In *The Cambridge Companion to Ezra Pound,* edited by Ira B. Nadel, 109–138. Cambridge: Cambridge University Press, 1999.

Cavanagh, Clare. *Osip Mandelstam and the Modernist Creation of Tradition.* Princeton, NJ: Princeton University Press, 1995.

Dante. "De Vulgari Eloquentia." In *Classical and Medieval Literary Criticism,* edited by A. Preminger, O. B. Hardison, Jr., and Kevin Kerraine. New York: Unger, 1974.

De Man, Paul. "Intentional Structure of the Romantic Image." In *Romanticism and Consciousness,* edited by Harold Bloom, 65–77. New York: Norton, 1970.

———. *Resistance to Theory.* Minneapolis, MN: University of Minnesota Press, 1986.

Derzhavin, Gavrila. *Poetic Works: A Bilingual Album.* Translated by Alexander Levitsky and Martha T. Kitchen. Providence, RI: Brown University, 2001.

———. *Stihotvoreniia* [Poems]. Leningrad: Sovetskii pisatel', 1957.

Donoghue, Denis. "The Human Image in Yeats." In *William Butler Yeats: A Collection of Criticism,* edited by Patrick J. Keane, 100–18. New York: McGraw-Hill, 1973.

———. *The Ordinary Universe: Soundings in Modern Literature.* New York: Macmillan, 1968.

Etkind, Efim. "Osip Mandelstam—Trilogiia o veke" [Osip Mandelstam—A trilogy about a century]. In *Slovo i sud'ba. Osip Mandel'shtam* [Word and Fate. Osip Mandelstam], 200–270. Moskva: Nauka, 1991.

Freidin, Gregory. *A Coat of Many Colors: Osip Mandelstam and His Mythologies of Self-Presentation.* Berkeley, CA: University of California Press, 1985.

Florenskii, Pavel. "Ikonostas" [Iconostasis]. In his *Collected Works,* vol. 1, 193–316. Paris: YMCA-Press, 1985.

Frye, Northrop. *Anatomy of Criticism.* Princeton, NJ: Princeton University Press, 1957. Reprinted New York: Atheneum, 1967.

————. *The Stubborn Structure.* Ithaca, NY: Cornell University Press, 1970.

Gasparov, Mikhail L. *Grazhdanskaia lirika Mandel'shtama 1937* [Mandelstam's civic poetry, 1937]. Moscow: Rossiiskii gosudarstvennyi gumanitarnyi universitet, 1996.

————. "'Solominka' Mandel'shtama: Poetika chernovika" [Mandelstam's "Little straw." The poetics of a draft copy]. In his *Izbrannye stat'i* [Selected essays], 185–197. Moscow: NLO, 1995.

Gasparov, Mikhail and Omri Ronen, "O 'Venitseiskoi zhizni' O. Mandel'shtama" [On 'Venetian life' of O. Mandelstam]. *Zvezda* 2, 2002: 193-2002.

Hansen-Löve, Aage. "Mandel'shtam's Thanatopoetics." In *Readings in Russian Modernism: To Honor Vladimir Fedorovich Markov*, edited by Ronald Vroon and John Malmstad, 121–157. Los Angeles, CA: University of California Press, 1993.

Hatlen, Burton. "Pound and Nature: Reading of Canto XXIII." *Paideuma* 25, nos. 1–2 (Spring and Fall 1996): 161–188.

Iakobson, Roman. "Poeziia grammatiki i grammatika poezii" [Grammar of poetry and poetry of grammar]. In his *Poetyca* [Poetics], 397–417. Warsaw: Polska Akademia Nauk, Institut Badań Literackich and Państwowe Wydawnictwo Naukove, 1961.

Ivanov, Viacheslav Ivanovich. *Liki i lichiny Rossii. Estetika i literaturnaia teoriia* [Russia's faces and masks. Esthetics and literary theory]. Moscow: Iskusstvo, 1995.

Ivanov, Viacheslav Vsevolodovich. "'Stikhi o neizvestnom soldate' v kontekste mirovoi poezii" ["Verses on the unknown soldier" in the context of world poetry]. In *Zhizn' i tvorchestvo O. E. Mandel'shtama* [Life and works of O. E. Mandelstam], 356-366. Voronezh: Voronezhskii gosudarstvennyi universitet, 1990.

————. *Izbrannye trudy po semiotike i istorii kul'tury* [Selected works on semiotics and the history of culture]. Vol. 2. Moscow: Yazyki russkoi kul'tury, 2000.

Jeffares, Alexander Norman. *W. B. Yeats: A New Biography.* New York: Farrar, Straus and Giroux, 1989.

————. *A New Commentary on the Poems of W. B. Yeats.* Stanford, CA: Stanford University Press, 1984.

————. *The Critical Heritage.* London: Routledge & Kegan, 1977.

————. *W. B. Yeats: Man and Poet.* London: Routledge & Kegan, 1962.

Keane, Patrick J. "Embodied Song." In *William Butler Yeats: A Collection of Criticism*, edited by Patrick J. Keane, 20–38. New York: McGraw-Hill, 1973.

Kearns, George. *Guide to Ezra Pound's Selected Cantos.* New Brunswick, NJ: Rutgers University Press, 1980.

Keats, John. *Poetical Works.* Edited by H. W. Garrod. Oxford: Oxford University Press, 1956. Reprinted 1987.

Kenner, Hugh. *The Pound Era.* Berkeley, CA: University of California Press, 1971.

Kern, Stephen. *The Culture of Time and Space.* Cambridge, MA: Harvard University Press, 1983.

Kovaleva, Irina, and Anton Nesterov. "Pindar i Mandel'shtam (K postanovke problemy) " [Pindar and Mandelstam (To the Formulation of the Problem)]. In *Mandel'shtam i antichnost'* [Mandelstam and classical antiquity], 166–168. Moscow: Rossiiskii gosudarstvennyi gumanitarnyi universitet, 1995.

Kulik, Alexander, "'Znacheniie svetlo': kliuch k 'Venitseiskoi zhizni' Osipa Mandel'shtama"[The meaning is light: key to "Venetian life by Osip Mandelstam]. *Wiener Slavistiches Jahrbuch* 3 (2015): 103-134.

Lawton, Anna, and Herbert Eagle, eds. and trans. *Russian Futurism through Its Manifestoes, 1912-1928.* Ithaca, NY: Cornell University Press, 1988.

Lawton, Anna, ed. *Russkii futurism* [The Russian futurism]. Moscow: Nasledie, 1999.

Leontiev, Konstantin. "Vizantizm i slavianstvo" [Bysantiumism and the Slavic world]. In *Vostok, Rossiia, Slavianstvo* [The Orient, Russia, the Slavic world], 94–155. Moscow: Respublika, 1996.

Letopis' zhizni i tvorchestva O. E. Mandel'stama [The chronicle of life and work of O. E. Mandelstam]. Compiled by A. G. Mets with particaption of S. V. Vasilenko, L. M. Vidgof, D. I. Zubarev, E. I. Lubiannikova, P. Mitzner. Saint Petersburg: Internet Edition, 2019.

Levin, Iurii. "Zametki o 'krymsko-ellinskikh stikhakh' O. Mandel'shtama" [Notes on O. Mandelstam's "Crimean–Hellenic verses"]. In *Mandel'shtam i antichnost'* [Mandelstam and classical antiquity], 77–103. Moscow: Rossiiskii gosudarstvennyi gumanitarnyi universitet, 1995.

———. "Zametki o poezii Mandel'shtama 30-kh godov. II. 'Stikhi o neizvestnom soldate'" [Notes on Mandelstam's poetry of the 30s. II. "Verses on the unknown soldier"]. *Slavica Hierosolymitana* 4 (1979): 185–212.

Lipkin, S. I. "Vtoraia doroga" [The second road]. In *K verkhov'iam* [Upstream], by Arkadii Shteinberg, 357–367. Moscow: Sovpadeniie, 1997.

Lotman, Iurii. "Zametki po poetike Tiutcheva" [Notes on Tiutchev's poetics]. In *O poetakh i poezii* [On poets and poetry], 553–564. St. Petersburg: Iskusstvo, 1996.

Lovejoy, Arthur O., and George Boas. *Primitivism and Related Ideas in Antiquity.* Baltimore, MD: John Hopkins Press, 1935.

Mandelstam, Nadezhda. *Hope against Hope.* New York: Charles Scribner, 1970.

——— [Mandel'shtam, Nadezhda]. "Kommentarii k stikham 1930–1937 gg." [Commentaries to the poems of 1930–1937]. In *Zhizn' i tvorchestvo O. E. Mandel'shtama* [Life and works of O. E. Mandelstam], 189–312. Voronezh: Voronezhskii gosudarstvennyi universitet, 1990.

——— [Mandel'shtam, Nadezhda]. *Vospominania* [Recollections]. Moscow: Soglasie, 1999.

——— [Mandel'shtam, Nadezhda]. *Vtoraia kniga* [Second book]. Moscow: Moskovskii rabochii, 1990.

——— [Mandel'shtam, Nadezhda]. *Tret'ia kniga* [Third book]. Moscow: Agraf, 2006.

Marinetti, Filippo. "The Foundation and the Manifesto of Futurism." In *Documents of 20th Century Art: Futurist Manifestos*, edited by Umbro Apollonio, translated by Robert Brain, R. W. Flint, J. C. Higgitt, and Caroline Tisdall, 19–24. New York: Viking Press, 1973. Originally published in *Le Figaro* (February 20, 1909).

Mikushevich, Vladimir. "Printsip sinkhronii v pozdnem tvorchestve Mandelstama" [Principle of sinchronicity in Mandelstam's later works] In *Zhizn' i tvorchestvo O. E. Mandel'shtama* [Life and works of O. E. Mandelstam], 427–437. Voronezh: Voronezhskii gosudarstvennyi universitet, 1990.

———. "Poeticheskii motiv i kontekst" [Poetic motive and context]. In *Voprosy teorii hudozhestvennogo perevoda* [On the theory of translating fiction], 40–42. Moscow: Khudozhestvennaia literatura, 1971.

———. "Dvoinaia dusha poeta v 'Grifel'noi ode' Mandel'shtama" [Double soul of the poet in Mandelstam's "Slate ode"], in *Sokhrani moiu rech'* [Preserve my speech] 3, no. 1 (2000).

Mets, Aleksandr. *Osip Mandel'shtam i ego vremia: Analiz tekstov* [Osip Mandelstam and his time: Text analysis]. St. Petersburg: n. p., 2011.

Moore, Virginia. *The Unicorn: William Butler Yeats's Search for Reality*. New York: Octagon Books, 1973.

Nielson, N. A. "Bessonnitsa" [Insomnia]. In *Mandel'shtam i antichnost'* [Mandelstam and classical antiquity], 65–76. Moscow: Rossiiskii gosudarstvennyi gumanitarnyi universitet, 1995.

Ortega y Gasset, José. *The Dehumanization of Art and Other Essays on Art, Culture, and Literature*. Princeton, NJ: Princeton University Press, 1968.

Ovid. *Metamorphoses*. Translated by A. D. Melville. Oxford, Oxford University Press, 1987. Reprinted New York: World's Classics Paperbacks, 1989.

Pasternak, Boris. *Sobranie sochinenii v piati tomakh* [Collected works in five volumes]. Moscow: Khudozhestvennaia literatura, 1989.

Poggioli, Renato. *The Theory of the Avant-Garde*. Cambridge, MA: The Belknap Press of Harvard University Press, 1968.

Pound, Ezra. *The Cantos of Ezra Pound*. London: Faber & Faber, 1975.

———. *The Cantos of Ezra Pound*. New York: New Directions, 1972.

———. *Gaudier-Brzeska: A Memoir*. New York: New Directions, 1970.

———. *Collected Shorter Poems*. London: Faber, 1968.

———. *ABC of Reading*. New York: New Directions, 1960.

————. *Literary Essays.* Edited and with an introduction by T. S. Eliot. London: Faber & Faber, 1954. Reprinted 1985.

————. *The Spirit of Romance.* Norfolk, CT: New Directions, 1953.

————. *Personnae: Collected Shorter Poems.* London: Faber, 1952.

————. *Personae: The Collected Poems of Ezra Pound.* New York: New Directions, 1950.

————. *Personae: The Collected Poems of Ezra Pound.* New York: Boni & Liveright, 1926.

Probstein, Ian. *The River of Time: Space, Time, History, and Language in Avant-Garde, Modernist, and Contemporary Russian and Anglo-American Poetry.* Boston: Academic Studies Press, 2017. https://www.academicstudiespress.com/jewsofrussiaeasterneurope/the-river-of-time?rq=The%20River%20of%20Time.

————, transl. Translations of "Stikhi o neizvestnom soldate," "Ya proshu kak zhalosti i milosti," "Ya skazhu eto nacherno shëpotom," "Mozhet byt' eto tochka bezumiia," "Chtob priyatel' i vetra i kapel'," "Na menya natselilas' grusha da cheremukha," by Osip Mandelstam. *Four Centuries of Russian Poetry in Translation* 4 (2013): 14–20. http://www.perelmuterverlag.de/FC42013.pdf.

————. "Fear and Awe: On Osip Mandelstam's 'The Slate Ode.'" Translation of "The Slate Ode" by Osip Mandelstam. *Brooklyn Rail: In Translation* (March 2011). http://intranslation.brooklynrail.org/russian/the-slate-ode.

————, transl. Translations of "Do not Tempt Foreign Tongues," "Ariosto," and "The Octaves," by Osip Mandelstam. *Brooklyn Rail: In Translation* (March 2011). http://intranslation.brooklynrail.org/russian/octaves-and-other-poems-by-osip-mandelstam.

————, transl. Translation of "Armenia. The Complete Cycle," by Osip Mandelstam. *Interlitq* 13 (November 2010). http://www.interlitq.org/issue13-2/osip-mandelstam/job.php.

————. "Nature and 'Paradiso Terrestre': Nature, Reality and Language in Pound, Yeats, and Mandelstam." *The McNeese Review* 46 (2008): 54–74.

————, transl. Translations of "Hagia Sophia" and "Impressionism," by Osip Mandelstam.In *Osip Mandelstam: New Translations,* edited by Ilya Bernstein, 6, 19. New York: Ugly Duckling Presse, 2006.

————, transl. Translations of "Hagia Sophia," "I Will Say It in Draft, In a Whisper," "Armed sith a Vision of Narrow Wasps," "I Will Tell You This, My Lady," by Osip Mandelstam. *International Poetry Review* 30, no. 2 (Fall 2004): 64–69.

————. "Three translations of Osip Mandelstam's 'Stalin's Epigram' with Selected Translations." *Jacket–2,* edited by Charles Bernstein: http://jacket2.org/commentary/ian-probstein-mandelstam.

Przybylski, Ryszard. *An Essay on the Poetry of Osip Mandelstam: God's Grateful Guest.* Translated by Madeline G. Levine. Ann Arbor, MI: Ardis, 1987.

——— [Pshybylski, Ryshard]. "Rim Osipa Mandelstama" [Osip Mandelstam's Rome]. In *Mandelstam i antichnost'* [Mandelstam and classical antiquity], 33–64. Moscow: Rossiiskii gosudarstvennyi gumanitarnyi universitet, 1995.

Robinson, Fred C. "'The Might of the North': Pound's Anglo-Saxon Studies and 'The Seafarer.'" *The Yale Review* 71 (1981–82): 199–224.

Ronen, Omry. *An Approach to Mandelstam.* Jerusalem: The Magnes Press, 1983.

——— [Ronen, Omri]. "K siuzhetu 'Stikhov o neizvestnom soldate' Mandel'shtama" [On the plot of the "Verses on the unknown soldier"]. *Slavica Hierosolymitana* 4 (1979): 214–222.

———. "Lexical Repetition, Subtext and Meaning in Osip Mandelstam's Poetics." In *Slavic Poetics: Essays in Honor of Kiril Taranovsky,* edited by Roman Jakobson, C. H. van Schooneveld, and Dean S. Worth, 49–66. Paris: Mouton, 1973.

Rosenthal, M. L. "A Critical Introduction" to *The Modern Poets.* Oxford: Oxford University Press, 1960. Reprinted as "Poems of Here and There" in *William Butler Yeats: A Collection of Criticism.* Edited by Patrick J. Keane. New York: McGraw-Hill, 1973.

Semenko, Irina M. *Poetika pozdnego Mandel'stama* [Mandelstam's later poetics]. Reprint ed. Moscow: Mandel'shtamovskoe obshchestvo, 1997.

———. "Tvorcheskaia istoriia 'Stikhov o neizvestnom soldate'" [History of the creation of "Verses on the unknown soldier"]. In *Zhizn' i tvorchestvo O. E. Mandel'shtama* [Life and works of O. E. Mandelstam], 479–505. Voronezh: Voronezhskii gosudarstvennyi universitet, 1990.

Schwartz, Sanford. *The Matrix of Modernism: Pound, Eliot, and Early Twentieth Century Thought.* Princeton, NJ: Princeton University Press, 1985.

Shattuck, Roger. *The Banquet Years.* New York: Vintage, 1968.

Shelley, Percy Bysshe. "A Defence of Poetry." In *Shelley's Poetry and Prose,* edited by Donald H. Reiman and Sharon B. Powers. New York: Norton, 1977.

———. *Poetical Works.* Edited by Thomas Hutchinson with corrections by G. M. Matthews. Oxford: Oxford University Press, 1970.

Shteinberg, Arkadii. *K verkhov'iam* [Upstream]. Moscow: Sovpadeniie, 1997.

Steiner, George. *After Babel: Aspects of Language and Translation.* Oxford: Oxford University Press, 1975.

Surat, Irina. "On Osip Mandelstam's Poem 'Impressionism.'" *Studia Literaturum* 6, no. 3 (2021): 166–183.

Surette, Leon. *The Birth of Modernism: Ezra Pound, T. S. Eliot, W. B. Yeats and the Occult.* Montreal: McGill-Queen's University Press, 1993.

Surette, Leon. *Light from Eleusis: A Study of the Cantos of Ezra Pound.* Oxford: Clarendon, 1979.

Taranovsky, Kiril. *Essays on Mandelstam*. Cambridge, MA: Harvard University Press, 1976.

——— [Taranovskii, Kirill]. *O poezii i poetike* [On poetry and poetics]. Moscow: Iazyki russkoi kul'tury, 2000.

——— [Taranovskii, Kirill]. "Tri zametki o poezii Mandel'shtama" [Three commentaries on Mandelstam's poetry]. *International Journal of Slavic Linguistics and Poetics* 12 (1969): 165–170.

Terras, Victor. "Osip Mandelstam and His Philosophy of the Word." In *Slavic Poetics: Essays in Honor of Kiril Taranovsky*, edited by Roman Jakobson, C. H. van Schooneveld, and Dean S. Worth, 455–461. Paris: Mouton, 1973.

Terrell, Carroll F. *A Companion to the Cantos of Ezra Pound*. Berkeley, CA: University of California Press, 1993.

Tiutchev, F. *Lirika. Stikhotvoreniia* [Lyric poetry]. 2 vols. Edited and compiled by Kirill V. Pigarev. Moscow: Nauka, 1965.

Tomashevskii, Boris. *Teoriia literatury: Poetika* [Theory of literature. Poetics]. Moscow: Aspekt Press, 1999.

Toporov, Viktor, ed. *T .S. Eliot: Polye liudi* [T .S. Eliot: Hollow men]. St. Petersburg: Kristall, 2000.

Toporov, Vladimir. *Enei—chelovek sud'by* [Aeneus—the man of fate]. Moscow: Radiks, 1993.

———. *Mif. Ritual. Simvol. Obraz. Issledovaniia v oblasti mifopoeticheskogo* [Myth. Ritual. Symbol. Image. Research in the sphere of the mythopoetic]. Moscow: Progress, 1995.

Tynianov, Iurii. "Promezhutok" [Gap]. In *Poetika. Istoriya Literatury. Kino* [Poetics. History of Literature. Cinema]. Moscow: Nauka, 1977.

———. *Problema stikhotvornogo iazyka* [Problem of the verse language]. Moscow: Sovetskii pisatel', 1965.

——— [Tynianov, Yuri]. "Problem of the Verse Language." In *Readings in Russian Poetics. Formalist and Structuralist Views*. Edited by Ladyslav Matejka and Krystyna Pomorska. Ann Arbor, MI: Michigan University Press, 1978.

Unterecker, John. *A Reader's Guide to W. B. Yeats*. New York: The Noonday Press, 1959.

Vallejo, César. "Telúrica y Magnética" [Teluric and Magnetic]. Poemario.org. https://poemario.org/poeta/cesar-vallejo/.

———. *The Complete Poetry. A Bilingual Edition*. Edited and translated by Clayton Eshleman. Berkeley, CA: University of California Press, 2007.

Ward, Bernadette Waterman. *World as Word. Philosophical Theology in Gerard Manley Hopkins*. Washington, DC: The Catholic Univerity of America Press, 2002.

Whitaker, Thomas. *Swan and Shadow: Yeats's Dialogue with History.* Chapel Hill, NC: University of North Carolina Press, 1964.

Wilhelm, James J. *The Later Cantos of Ezra Pound.* New York: Walker, 1977.

Yeats, William Butler. *The Collected Poems of W. B. Yeats.* Edited by Richard J. Finneran. New York: Macmillan, 1989.

Zhirmunskii, Viktor. "Preodolevshiie simvolism" [Those who overcame symbolism]. In his *Poetika russkoi poezii* [Poetics of the Russian poetry], 364–404. St. Petersburg: Azbuka–klassika, 2001.

Алфавитный указатель стихотворений

1 января 1924 — 29-30, 48, 49, 59, 134

10 января 1934 (вариант 2) — 232

«Ах, ничего я не вижу, и бедное ухо оглохло…» — 146

А небо будущим беременно… — 29, 130

Айя-София — 43, 84

Ариост — 204

Армения — 144

Батюшков — 200

«В год тридцать первый от рожденья века…» — 182

«В игольчатых чумных бокалах…» — 222

Век — 29, 48-49, 112

«Веницейской жизни, мрачной и бесплодной…» — 35–37, 106

«Вернись в смесительное лоно…» — 104

«Вооружённый зреньем узких ос…» — 254

Восьмистишия — 214

«Гончарами велик остров синий…» — 27, 274

Грифельная ода — 30, 54-65, 71, 122

«Дайте Тютчеву стрекóзу…» — 202

«Дано мне тело — что мне делать с ним…» —78

Декабрист — 92

«День стоял о пяти головах. Сплошные пять суток…» — 238

«Дикая кошка — армянская речь…» — 166

«Длинной жажды должник виноватый…» — 276

«Дрожжи мира дорогие…» — 250

«Дышали шуб меха. Плечо к плечу теснилось…» — 230

«Есть женщины, сырой земле родные…» — 284

«Ещё далёко мне до патриарха…» — 186

«Ещё мы жизнью пóлны в высшей мере…» — 240

«Ещё не умер ты. Ещё ты не один…» — 250

«За гремучую доблесть грядущих веков…» — 28, 170

«За Паганини длиннопалым…» — 37, 242

«За то, что я руки твои не сумел удержать…» — 108

«Закутав рот, как влажную розу…» — 150

«Захочешь жить, тогда глядишь с улыбкой…» — 184

«И клёна зубчатая лапа…» — 220

«И Шуберт на воде, и Моцарт в птичьем гаме…» — 220

«И я выхожу из пространства…» — 55, 224

Импрессионизм — 35, 198

«Исполню дымчатый обряд…» — 244

«К пустой земле невольно припадая… — 284

«Как люб мне натугой живущий…» — 164

«Какая роскошь в нищенском селеньи…» — 154

«Квартира тиха, как бумага…» — 208

«Когда в тёплой ночи замирает…» — 94

«Когда душе столь торопкой, столь робкой…» — 230

«Когда, уничтожив набросок…» — 218

«Колючая речь Араратской долины…» — 162

«Лазурь да глина, глина да лазурь…» — 156

Ламарк — 21-22, 194

«Лишив меня морей, разбега и разлёта…» — 25, 236

«Люблю появление ткани…» — 214

«Меня преследуют две-три случайных фразы…» — 228

«Может быть, это точка безумия…» — 268

«Мы живём, под собою не чуя страны…» — 72-76, 212

«На каменных отрогах Пиэрии…» — 26, 100

«…На луне не растёт…» — 86

«На меня нацелилась груша да черёмуха…» — 282

«На полицейской бумаге верже…» — 158

Нашедший подкову — 30, 47-52, 59-61, 71, 116

«Не говори никому…» — 160

«Не искушай чужих наречий, но постарайся их забыть…» — 206

«Не развалины — нет! — но порубка могучего циркульного леса…» — 152

«Не сравнивай: живущий несравним…» — 270

«Не у меня, не у тебя — у них…» — 20, 23, 246

Неправда — 174

«Нереиды мои, нереиды!…» — 278

«Нет, не спрятаться мне от великой муры…» — 172

«Нет, никогда, ничей я не был современник…» — 140

«О порфирные цокая граниты…» — 156

«О, бабочка, о, мусульманка…» — 216

«О, как же я хочу…» — 278

«Орущих камней государство…» — 152

Отрывки из уничтоженных стихов — 182

«Паденье — неизменный спутник страха…» — 82

«Полночь в Москве. Роскошно буддийское лето…» — 176

Посох — 88

«Преодолев затверженность природы…» — 218

«Прославим, братья, сумерки свободы…» — 96

«Пусти меня, отдай меня, Воронеж…» — 24, 236

«Римских ночей полновесные слитки…» — 240

«Руку платком обмотай и в венценосный шиповник…» — 150

«С розовой пеной усталости у мягких губ…» — 110

«Сегодня можно снять декалькомании…» — 190

«Сёстры — тяжесть и нежность, одинаковы ваши приметы…» — 102

[Стихи к Н<аталии> Е. Штемпель] — 284

«Скажи мне, чертёжник пустыни…» — 222

Стихи о неизвестном солдате — 30, 38, 256

Стихи памяти Андрея Белого — 226

Tristia — 98

«Ты красок себе пожелала…» — 148

«Ты розу Гафиза колышешь…» — 144

«Уж я люблю московские законы…» — 182

«Улыбнись, ягненок гневный с Рафаэлева холста…» — 248

«Уничтожает пламень…» — 90

Утро 10 января 1934 — 228
«Флейты греческой тэта и йота…» — 26, 280
«Холодно розе в снегу…» — 154
«Что делать нам с убитостью равнин…» — 252
«Чтоб, приятель и ветра и капель…» — 25, 272
«Шестого чувства крошечный придаток…» — 22-23, 216
«Я больше не ребенок! …» — 184
«Я буду метаться по табору улицы тёмной…» — 142
«Я должен жить, хотя я дважды умер…» — 236
«Я молю, как жалости и милости…» — 264
«Я ненавижу свет…» — 80
«Я скажу тебе с последней прямотой…» — 27, 168
«Я скажу это начерно, шёпотом…» — 266
«Я тебя никогда не увижу…» — 156
«Язык булыжника мне голубя понятней…» — 128

Alphabetical Index of Poems

A blue island, green Crete is extolled, 27, 275
A country of roaring stones, 153
A Decembrist, 93
A guilty debtor of a long-time thirst, 277
A living man's unique: do not compare, 271
A prickly speech of the Ararat Valley, 163
A rose is cold in the snow, 155
A tiny appendage of the sixth sense, 22-23, 217
A wild cat—the Armenian speech, 167
Ah, I can't see a thing, and my poor ear is deaf, 147
An apartment is quiet as paper, 209
And the jagged bough of a maple-tree, 221
And the Sky is Pregnant with the Future, 29, 131
Ariosto, 205
Armed with the vision of narrow wasps, 255
Armenia, 145
Azure and clay, clay and azure skies, 157
Batiushkov, 201
Because I could not hold your hands in mine, 109
Both Schubert on the water and Mozart in birds' chirping, 221
Clanking on regal granites, 157
Clearer than pigeon's talk to me is stone's tongue, 129
Covering your mouth like a dewy rose, 151
Do not tempt foreign tongues—attempt forgetting them, alas, 207
Don't tell it anyone—forget, 161
For the thunderous courage of ages to come, 28, 171

Give Tiutchev a dragonfly, 203
Go back to the incestuous womb, 105
Greek flute's theta and iota, 26, 281
Hagia Sophia, 43, 85
Hail, brothers, let us praise our freedom's twilight, 97
Having deprived me of seas, flight, and space, 25, 237
How dear to me are those people, 165
I am far from being as old as patriarch, 187
I am given a body—what should I, 79
I am haunted by a couple of random phrases, 229
I am no longer a child!, 185
I beg like compassion and grace, 265
I hate the light, 81
I have already loved Moscow laws, 183
I have to live though I died twice, 237
I like when the substance appears, 215
I will never see you again, 157
I will say it in draft and in whisper, 20, 267
I will tell you this, my lady, 27, 169
I'll fulfill a dim rite, 245
I'll rush along a gypsy camp of a dark street, 143
I'm under fire of a bird cherry tree and a pear tree, 283
If you are thirsty, then look with a smile, 185
Impressionism, 35, 199
It might be the point of insanity, 269
It's such a luxury in a poor village, 155
January 1, 1924, 29-30, 48, 49, 59, 135
January 10, 1934 (version 2), 233
Lamarck, 21-22, 195
Let go, Voronezh, raven-town, 24, 237
Midnight in Moscow. A Buddhist summer is lavish, 177
My nereids, oh, my nereids!, 279
No, I won't be able to hide from a great mess, 173
No, I've never been anyone's contemporary, 141
…Not a single blade, 87
Not I, not you—but they, 20, 23, 247
Not ruins—no, but a cutting-down of a mighty circular wood, 153
Octaves, 215
Oh, how I madly crave, 279
Oh, Moslem-butterfly, 217
On steep stony ridges of Pieria, 26, 101
On the police laid paper the night, 159
On the thirty-first year from this century's birth, 183
Overcoming the hardiness of nature, 219
[Poems for N<atalia> E. Shtempel], 285
Sisters, heaviness and tenderness, your traits are akin, 103
Smile, angry lamb from Rafael's canvas, don't rage, 249
So I leave space for a wild garden, 55, 225
Solid gold bars of the Roman nights, 241
Some women are kin to damp earth, 285
Tell me, a draftsman of the desert, 223

The Age, 29, 48-49, 113
The day was five-headed: five unbreakable days, 239
The fall is a constant companion of fear, 83
The fire destroys, 91
The furs of coats breathed, shoulder to shoulder, 231
The Horseshoe Finder, 30, 47-52, 59-61, 71, 117
The meaning of fruitless and gloomy, 35–37, 107
The Morning of January 10, 1934, 229
The Slate Ode, 30, 54-65, 71, 123
The Wand, 89
They run like a gypsy throng, 37, 243
To help a friend of rain and wind, 25, 273
To the Memory of Andrei Bely, 227
Today we can take decals, 191
Tristia, 99
Untruth, 175
Unwillingly clinging to a bare land, 285
Verses on the Unknown Soldier, 30, 38, 257
We are still sentenced to life, 241
We drink the enchantment of causes, 223
We live without feeling our country's pulse, 72-76, 213
What should we do with murdered plains, 253
When a feverish forum of Moscow, 95
When a soul, impatient, shy and fast, 231
When having destroyed your draft, 219
With the pink foam of fatigue around soft lips, 111
World's golden yeast, our dear, 251
Wrap your hand in a handkerchief and boldly, 151
You haven't died yet. You are not alone, 251
You rock the rose of Hafiz, 145
You wished colors—and then, 149

Ian Probstein, professor of English at Touro College, has published numerous books and articles. In all, about 500 publications. His most recent book in English is *The River of Time: Time-Space, History, and Language in Avant-Garde, Modernist, and Contemporary Russian and Anglo-American Poetry* (Boston: Academic Studies Press, 2017), http://www.academicstudiespress.com/browse-catalog/the-river-of-time, and in Russian, translations in the annotated edition of T. S. Eliot's *The Waste Land. The Hollow Men. Poetry and Plays* (St. Petersburg: Azbuka–Antikva, 2018), and translation of the *Sign Under Test: Selected Poems and Essays* by Charles Bernstein (Moscow: Russkii Gulliver, 2020), shortlisted for the Russian Translation Guild Master Award. His essays, poems in English, and translations of poetry into English have been published in *Atlanta Review, The International Literary Quarterly, Brooklyn Rail: In Translation, Jacket-2, Four Centuries of Russian Poetry in Translation, Osip Mandelstam. New Translations* (New York: Ugly Duckling Presse, 2006), and *International Poetry Review, Salonika, Spring* (a journal of E. E. Cummings Society), *Calliope, CrazyHorse, Rhino, Sibilla, Circumference, The Epoch Times, The McNeese Review, Metamorphosis, Slavic Review*, and some others as well as in *A Bilingual Anthology of the Contemporary Russian Free Verse* (Moscow: Online publication, 2021 https://en.rusfreeverse.com/ian-probshtein-en; both as an author and as a translator into English), *An Anthology of Jewish-Russian Literature, 1801–2001: Two Centuries of a Dual Identity*, 2 vols., ed. Maxim D. Shrayer (Armonk, NY: M. E. Sharpe, 2007), vol. 2, and in the book *Vita Nuova* (Philadelphia: R. E. M. Press, 1992).

CPSIA information can be obtained
at www.ICGtesting.com
Printed in the USA
JSHW030841110522
25806JS00003B/3